To Barbara & Ki——
This just goes to show
you what kicking, crying
and stamping of feet can do—
                Much love —
                    Marian

BOOKS BY MARIAN KLAMKIN

Flower Arranging for Period Decoration
Flower Arrangements that Last
The Collector's Book of Art Nouveau
The Collector's Book of Bottles
The Collector's Book of Boxes
The Collector's Book of Wedgwood

Frontispiece
TOP LEFT *White jasper vase with lilac and green relief*
TOP RIGHT *Fairyland lustre shows transluscent with light placed inside.*
BOTTOM LEFT *Pearlware oblong serving dish; c.1835*
BOTTOM RIGHT *Pair of 'Dragon Lustre' vases. Blue mottled glaze with gold-printed dragons.*

The Collector's Book of
WEDGWOOD

MARIAN KLAMKIN

Illustrated with photographs by Charles Klamkin

DODD, MEAD & COMPANY · NEW YORK

First published in the United States in 1971

All rights reserved

ISBN 0–396–06368–3

Library of Congress Catalog Card Number: 70–154063

Printed in Great Britain

Contents

Acknowledgements

Without the encouragement, co-operation and aid of many Wedgwood devotees, both collectors and dealers, in England and America this effort would have been most difficult. The author is grateful for the help of Mr and Mrs Joseph Blum, Mr and Mrs Ludy Spero, Mr and Mrs Nick Bonadeis, Mr and Mrs Leo Kaplan, Mr and Mrs John A. Coe, and Mr and Mrs Alexander Schaffer.

The late Mr Harry M. Buten has also been most helpful and encouraging in sharing his enthusiasm and in sending needed information from the Buten Museum of Wedgwood in Merion, Pennsylvania. The author thanks Mr Paul F. Rovetti and Mr William H. Watkins of the Mattatuck Historical Society, Waterbury, Connecticut, for allowing the Mattatuck Museum's collection of Wedgwood to be photographed. Mr Simon S. Jervis, Assistant Keeper of Furniture and Woodwork, Victoria and Albert Museum, sent needed information, as did Miss Judith Turner, Press Officer of Wedgwood in London.

Others who deserve recognition and the author's gratitude are Mrs Jane Ricks King, Mr Gil Kahn, Miss Charlotte Spungin, Miss Clare Leighton, Mr James Oliver Brown, Mr Allen T. Klots, Jr, and Mr Murray Pollinger.

1
Introduction

The popularity of Josiah Wedgwood's pottery has fluctuated several times since the end of the eighteenth century when his neo-classic designs were generally accepted as the epitome of good taste. The simple elegance of Wedgwood's jasperware, so different from the over-decorated rococo pottery and porcelain that preceded it, gave it great popularity in Wedgwood's own time. Interest lagged towards the middle of the nineteenth century, but towards its end collectors once again discovered Wedgwood's genius.

The jasperware always associated with the name of Wedgwood is not the only pottery for which he has been remembered. Through his improvements and perfection of creamware and successful use of this clay body to make kitchen and table ware for the emerging middle classes, who could not afford the hand-made porcelain dishes available in the eighteenth century, he made a lasting contribution to Western civilisation. His inventiveness marked the end of hand-produced pottery for the wealthy few by providing fine wares for all.

Wedgwood found the secret of mass production without compromising quality—his main claim to fame. His desire for perfection and his ability to achieve it left the

Creamware tea canister with cover. Transfer decorated in black. Marked: Wedgwood. C1775. Height, 5½in. [Spero Collection]

Basalt bust of Winston Churchill, modelled by Arnold Machin, 1940. Height, 6in. [Jo-Anne Blum, inc]

world with a vast amount and variety of ceramics. The combination of quality and quantity in Wedgwood products has made them the most collectable of all ceramics.

No one, it seems, can become a casual collector of Wedgwood. The possession of one fine plaque or vase leads to the desire for another. Fortunately, 200 years has produced plenty for the collector, and, indeed, it is almost necessary for him to specialise in one type or period of Wedgwood pottery. From the days of its founder the Wedgwood firm has produced useful and decorative pottery in great numbers in an infinite variety of shapes, colours and clay bodies.

Some categories of old Wedgwood have become too scarce and expensive for most collectors, but there are still types other than the early jasperware, basalt and agate ware that are highly collectable and can still be found. Eighteenth-century basalt busts and medallions and the exquisite jasper plaques and vases are the most desirable items, but, as we have said, they are rare and extremely expensive. Their value has risen enormously for the same reason that all good antiques increase in value: they possess intrinsic beauty and there are no more of comparable quality being made.

Although the Wedgwood factory has continued to produce large quantities of pottery since the days of its founder, it is eighteenth- and early nineteenth-century pottery that has always attracted the dedicated Wedgwood collector. This is not to say that certain Victorian and modern Wedgwood has not become collectable also. Josiah Wedgwood's philosophy of hiring the best available artists to design and decorate his pottery has continued as a tradition in the factory, which was family-run until recently. The careful, knowledgeable and sophisticated collector recognises and purchases when he can all Wedgwood that is representative of any decorative art period, whether old or new.

Nineteenth-century Wedgwood, for instance, long disdained by collectors as just reproducing the first Wedgwood's designs or representing the bad taste of the

Pair of plaques designed and modelled by Anna Zinkeisen in 1924, entitled 'Adam' and 'Eve'. Style is what has recently been categorised as 'Art Deco'. Light blue jasper with white relief. Diameter 5in. [Kaplan]

Victorians, has now come into its own. Along with other decorative articles of the Victorian period of eclecticism, nineteenth–century pottery and china have become highly collectable.

If one agrees that the quality of Wedgwood is usually superior to other contemporary pottery, then one can admire the Wedgwood made in the many styles prevalent in the nineteenth century. There are also many interesting collectable items made by Wedgwood in limited amounts in this century which are much sought after.

2
Josiah Wedgwood

To appreciate the quality of Wedgwood pottery, it is necessary to have some knowledge of the personality and philosophy of the founder of the company. Josiah Wedgwood was born in 1730 into a family that had been making pottery in the Staffordshire region of England for many generations, and learned potting early. His father died when the boy, the youngest of thirteen children, was only nine years old and this cut short Josiah's education. He went to work for his elder brother, Thomas, at the Churchyard Works, which seems to have been their only inheritance from their father, who had not been particularly successful. At the age of eleven Josiah suffered an attack of smallpox which made it necessary for him to give up the physical labour of throwing at the potter's wheel and to turn his talents and interest to modelling and making moulds. The disease had affected his right knee, and later in life he had to have his leg amputated.

After five years of apprenticeship to his brother, Josiah left the Churchyard Works and went into partnership with John Harrison, who made agate ware, but this partnership lasted only a short time and in 1754 he became a partner of Thomas Whieldon, who was an extremely talented and dedicated potter. This partnership enabled Wedgwood to experiment freely with clay bodies and glazes in order to improve the quality and appearance of English ceramics. We must remember that pottery was then partly hand-made and available only to those who were willing to

Wedgwood-Whieldon ware. Cauliflower-shaped teapot and sugarbox with covers. Green-glaze plate is typical Wedgwood shape. No marks. C1760. Plate is 10in diameter. [Mattatuck Museum]

Creamware milk pitcher, one of pair. Hand-painted in Anthemion pattern, red and black border. Shape is from 1815 catalogue and border pattern is # 75 from first pattern book. Height, 12in. [Schaffer Collection]

Creamware plate with dog's portrait in sepia. Marked: Wedgwood. 1878. Diameter, 8¾in. [Klamkin]

pay high prices for rather inferior quality. The better wares were imported from China and some of the European countries. The average household used woodenware, leather, pewter, and salt-glaze pottery from which to serve and eat. During Wedgwood's association with Thomas Whieldon, though their firm was fairly prosperous, the demand for more and better ware increased. Wedgwood was in sympathy with the need to find improved clay bodies and glazes and it was during this period that he invented a green glaze that was very successful, both artistically and commercially. Dishes in the shapes of fruit and vegetables were made from this ware and the green glaze is still popular. This early Whieldon-Wedgwood ware is not marked.

11

In 1759 Wedgwood, like most promising young men, went into business for himself. At the age of twenty-nine, with little capital, he leased part of an estate belonging to distant cousins in Burslem. These cousins, also potters, were successful but semi-retired, so he was able to take over the workrooms, sheds and kilns known as the Ivy House Works, where he continued to make the kind of wares he had made during his partnership with Whieldon. At that period he began to divide the labour among his workers, a very advanced practice for the time; he believed that regularity in quality and design could only come from each man being trained to do one job to the best of his ability. This was the beginning of mass production in the pottery industry in England.

Wedgwood's first major contribution to the world of ceramics and perhaps the most satisfying to him was his improvement of creamware—the cream-coloured light-bodied earthenware used mainly for useful tableware. His was the first light-bodied ware made and sold in quantity in Great Britain. Wedgwood presented a breakfast set to Queen Charlotte in 1762 and after 1765 was given royal permission to call it Queen's ware.

Queen's ware was sold all over the British Isles and Europe and large quantities of it were imported into the colonies in America. This American trade was interrupted only by the Revolutionary War, during which Wedgwood sympathised with the colonists.

Basalt paperweight in shape of Egyptian sphinx. Marked: Wedgwood. Eighteenth century. It is likely that Josiah Wedgwood himself modelled this shape. Length of base, 6in. [Klamkin]

Wedgwood and Bentley basalt rumpot. Although cover is missing, this photograph illustrates the fine patina on the basalt of this period. Marked: Wedgwood and Bentley. C1775. Height, 3½in. [Klamkin]

From 1768 to 1780 Wedgwood was in partnership with Thomas Bentley, a man of refinement and excellent taste who was interested only in the decorative wares with which Wedgwood had been experimenting (including jasperware and basalt). Bentley had been a close friend of Wedgwood before their partnership was formed and this friendship continued until Bentley's death in 1780. Bentley ran the London showroom and promoted the decorative wares while Wedgwood engaged his cousin, Thomas Wedgwood, to run the factory, called The Bell House, for useful ware. A factory was also built outside Burslem and called Etruria, and it was here that the neo-classic decorative wares were developed and made. In 1773 all the operations were moved to Etruria.

During the Wedgwood and Bentley partnership jasperware, black basalt, Queen's ware, drabware, redware, agate ware and many other types of ceramics were invented, designed or improved upon by Josiah Wedgwood. This was the finest period of design and quality that his factory enjoyed.

After Bentley's death production continued in both the decorative and useful wares, and jasperware vases were produced. The useful ware was by far the more profitable department and at times supported the production of the decorative pieces. Wedgwood's vast amount of experimentation on his jasperware products was extremely costly.

13

(above) *Blue jasper tablet, white relief. Subject: Birth of Bacchus. Very high relief and careful modelling shows this plaque to be of late eighteenth century or early nineteenth. Marked: Wedgwood. Length, 12in. Height, 5in.* [Klamkin];

(left) *Covered cup and saucer. Jasper, in blue, yellow and white. Engine-turned and applied bas-relief. Jasper dice-work was one of Josiah Wedgwood's finest accomplishments. Marked: Wedgwood. C1795. Height, 4½in.* [Spero Collection]

He became a wealthy man and died in 1795. He was a man born in the right era for the accomplishment that he sought and achieved. The style of his time, established by the enormous interest in classic form, was mainly due to the talent of Robert Adam, who, as architect-designer-decorator adapted the classic form to contemporary design. Wedgwood hired the best available artists to design decorative accessories for the classical-revival style and public acceptance compensated him for his efforts. This tradition of using the talents of accepted contemporary artists has continued throughout the 200 years of the Wedgwood company's existence.

Most of the literature available to the Wedgwood collector concerns eighteenth-century jasperware and basalt, which are not easily found today. Old Queen's ware and other clay bodies of the eighteenth century have, with the current interest in all eighteenth-century antiques, rocketed in price. However, the collector should know about these early pieces, for there may come a time when he will find one of them. Those who have been collecting Wedgwood for any length of time know that there is no end to the amount and different types of Wedgwood of periods later than that of the first Josiah that are still available.

Since eighteenth-century jasperware, basalt ware, early green glaze, and agate ware are so difficult to find, it is unlikely that the new collector will specialise in any of these, though there is still enough available for anyone who is building a comprehensive collection. Many collectors specialise in Wedgwood's Queen's ware by border patterns, or by subject matter of decoration such as flowers, crests, etc. Buttons, plaques, Victoriana, Majolica, miniature boxes, teapots, cups and saucers, flower containers, and jewellery, are all categories of collecting that can be exclusively or partly Wedgwood.

Majolica c o m p o t e. Basic colours blue and green. 'Somnus' motif forms the base. Late nineteenth c e n t u r y. Marked: Wedgwood, on base. Height, 11in. [Jo-Anne Blum, Inc]

3
The Wedgwood Collector

Without delving into the deep-seated human drive for acquisition, we all know people who are continually searching for one type of stamp, a special rare coin, a certain old theatre programme or a piece of eighteenth-century Wedgwood creamware with a particular border pattern. Wedgwood collectors are not always the most affluent of people attending auctions and haunting the antique shops, for there is much inexpensive old Wedgwood to be found. There have been Wedgwood collectors almost as long as there has been Wedgwood. In recent years, Queen's ware, long neglected by collectors and museums, has become more desirable, particularly in England, and the list of those specialising in Queen's ware in America is growing also.

Creamware footbath. Printed and hand-painted decoration. These formerly useful objects are becoming collector's items, particularly in America, where they are used decoratively. Marked: Wedgwood. Early nineteenth century. Length, 18½in. [Jo-Anne Blum, Inc]

16

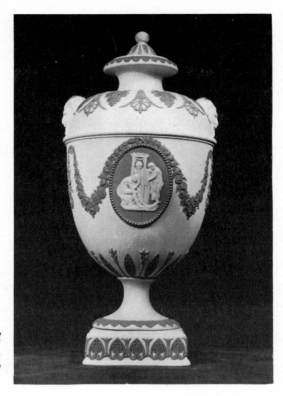

White jasper vase with lilac and green relief. Marked: Wedgwood. All three-colour jasper is desired by collectors. Height, 8½in. [Kaplan]

Wedgwood ware represents the history of the potter's art in the western world for the past 200 years. The Wedgwood firm has, since its founding, attempted to produce what the contemporary market demanded as well as continuing to make the classical designs that began in the days of its founder. A comprehensive collection of Wedgwood pottery has examples of neo-classic, empire, Victorian, art nouveau, oriental and contemporary art and these are often the best designed, decorated and executed of any particular kind of pottery made in the past 200 years to be found anywhere.

Because the output of the Wedgwood factory has always been enormous, it is possible to find almost anything one wants, which is one of the reasons that Wedgwood collecting has become so popular. There is little enjoyment in collecting something that is next to impossible to find. Also, the Wedgwood factory has always hired the best contemporary artists available, so much of its production consists of the art of the period. The experienced Wedgwood collector knows which pieces of new Wedgwood pottery are likely to become valuable and important as time goes on. For the neophyte collector we will examine some of these collectable categories later.

Other reasons for collecting are that Wedgwood pottery is prettier than stamps, more durable than porcelain, and much of it is useful; and there is usually some to be found in almost any country where one is likely to travel, but never so much

17

Plate with printed Chinese-inspired red and blue design. This ware and mark, 'Wedgwood's Stone China', are rarely found today and are prized by those collectors who search for examples of every type of pottery Wedgwood made. Diameter, 10in. [Jo-Anne Blum, Inc]

that hunting for it becomes boring. Wedgwood collecting is also a satisfying hobby for those who like to browse in antique shops and attend auctions.

Some Wedgwood collectors will purchase both new or old Wedgwood if it appeals to them. Many collectors watch for new work designed by particular contemporary artists whom they know design for Wedgwood. These designer pieces are often made in limited quantities and become very desirable very quickly. Other collectors purchase new jasperware when it is issued in a particular favourite colour and still others attempt to acquire an example of every colour that was ever made by Wedgwood.

There are, of course, many affluent collectors who buy only eighteenth- or early nineteenth-century jasperware and basalt, knowing that their collections will have both antique and artistic value. Good identifiable antiques always increase in value, especially if they are artistically important to begin with.

In addition to increasing in value with time, a collection of the best Wedgwood brings its owner more status among other collectors, which is one reason some people collect.

Wedgwood covers many decorative periods, as mentioned before, and this appeals to collectors. Those who specialise and are particularly interested in Victoriana will find Wedgwood plates and vases in the style of that ornate period. With a revival of interest in the period of art nouveau, there are collectors who have found the lustreware designed and decorated by Daisy Makeig-Jones between 1915 and 1932 an exciting combination of the art nouveau style and Chinese, Japanese and Persian influences. This lustreware has increased in value along with Tiffany glass and other innovative art glass and ceramics made in the same time.

The collector of blue and white transfer pattern ironstone will find excellent examples in Wedgwood, though it is scarcer than other makes. There are plates in Wedgwood pearlware that are typical of the cottage ware of the early nineteenth century. There are commemorative plates for collectors also, for in this century they have become an important part of Wedgwood's business. Even though most of these plates have no antique value, many of them are desirable because they are made in limited runs and are often designed by well known artists.

Many people collect any Wedgwood, old or new, so long as it is in their favourite colour. There are other collectors who buy only small jasper and basalt medallions, cameos and intaglios—wonderful items for the collector with limited space and an

(above) *Plate hand-decorated by Walter Crane, illustrator and artist, who worked for Wedgwood Company between 1867 and 1877. Length, 12in; (left) Mark on underside showing artist's monogram [Schaffer Collection]*

19

Advertising tile made for American importer of Wedgwood in Boston. These tiles, now popular as collector's items in USA, are collected in series. Sepia print. Front shows House of Seven Gables, Salem, Massachusetts and reverse, calendar year for 1929, the last year these tiles were made. Marked: Wedgwood (on outer edge). Many of the calendar tiles were not marked. Length, 6in. Width, 4in. [Klamkin]

unlimited pocketbook. Classical plaques are another collector's passion, while still others specialise in teapots or cups and saucers.

The Wedgwood collector who can limit himself to any of the above categories shows more willpower than the great majority of his fellows. At one time the supply of eighteenth- and early nineteenth-century Wedgwood was sufficient to satisfy most collectors, but it has become scarce and expensive enough in the past ten years to make searching for just one age or type very difficult and somewhat frustrating. Few collections are dispersed today through private sale or auctions. Many museums, which formerly gave little space to ceramics, now realise the artistic and historical importance of Wedgwood and are constantly searching for important pieces for their collections.

What, therefore, can the new collector find in Wedgwood today and what should he buy? First and foremost, search for early Queen's ware. Learn as much as you can about the typical shapes of the many plates that Wedgwood made and learn to recognise the border patterns and the typical pale cream glaze and body of this ware.

Another type of old Wedgwood that is still fairly abundant is pearlware. Some of the border patterns will be the same as those of Queen's ware, and though the white appearance of pearlware may not be as appealing to collectors as the cream-coloured plates, many of the dishes in the pearl glaze are quite lovely. While a majestic tureen in eighteenth-century creamware may not turn up in your neigh-

20

bourhood antique shop, you may, eventually, find a later one in pearlware just as decorative.

There is still a lot of nineteenth–century majolica to be found. The glazes are magnificent and the shapes are often quite pleasing. Wedgwood majolica is really Queen's ware in disguise, and for those who appreciate Victorian pottery, this is a field of collecting that is rewarding, fairly cheap, and with an excellent future.

Searching for the unusual in Wedgwood wares is yet another interesting category of Wedgwood collecting. There are always pieces of creamware, jasperware and basalt that require a certain amount of research before the purpose for which they were originally made can be discovered. Among these oddities are baby feeders, bidets, platter tilters, knife rests, conceits, cigar holders, sword hilts, beer keg handles, bell pulls, keyhole escutcheons, and many other articles, both useful and decorative, that Wedgwood developed and produced. His inventiveness and imagination led him to attempt to make any article he could possibly think of; but many, while innovative and practical in their own time, have been replaced by more functional, less aesthetic, articles today. The old non-practical Wedgwood is, therefore, mainly of historical importance, indicating the way people lived 200 years ago.

Wedgwood appeals to people of different tastes and interests and for many different reasons. Perhaps it is because there is so much variety in this one category of collecting that it is less competitive than many other kinds. Wedgwood collectors have formed organisations in order to pool their knowledge and further research in their field, which knowledge and research they willingly share with others.

Basalt bust of Shakespeare. These miniature busts in basalt are quite rare, though they have been made during several different periods. Marked: Wedgwood. Height, 4in.

4
Notes on Wedgwood Collecting

Often one's first purchase in Wedgwood is a piece of blue and white jasperware or blue jasper dip with white bas relief. Often, also, it is purchased simply because its buyer liked it, recognised it as Wedgwood and thought it was pretty. Often, also, as the collector becomes more sophisticated, these first purchases are put aside and other types of Wedgwood take their place. 'I didn't know Wedgwood made that!' is frequently heard at dealers' booths in antique shows and in the ceramics displays in museums. The piece which the uninformed do not recognise as Wedgwood is usually what is most collectable today.

No one should begin to collect without first investing in several good books on the subject, itself a separate phase of Wedgwood collecting. Do not invest too much money without being able to identify the age and category of the purchases. The Wedgwood collector must know where his piece fits into the Wedgwood story and whether it is, in truth, a collector's item.

Book rack of burl walnut with brass rope decoration. Wedgwood medallions in blue and white jasper set in sides. Mid-nineteenth century. Diameter of medallions, 1¾ in. [Klamkin]

(left) *'Ivanhoe' pattern pearlware plate. Printed and hand-decorated over the glaze. Titled: 'Rebecca repelling the Templar'. Marked: Wedgwood, Etruria, England, P, and 'Ivanhoe'. Many of these plates were made, but hand-painted examples are rare. Diameter, 10in. [Klamkin];* (right) *Pearlware plate with Russian motifs as decoration. Printed and hand-painted over the glaze. Marked: Wedgwood, Etruria, England, P. Diameter, 10in. [Klamkin]*

After the fledgling collector has read enough books and, most particularly, looked at enough photographs, he will begin to recognise pieces of early Queen's ware, become acquainted with eighteenth-century border patterns, congratulate himself when he turns over a piece of well made majolica, be able to spot the Wedgwood mark on an old butter mould and develop an eye for the shapes that are typical Wedgwood. The experienced collector is able to pick out a piece of Wedgwood among scores of other plates, dishes or bowls as though a ray of light were pointing directly to it. This ability to spot Wedgwood, even some of the more esoteric items, comes only with knowledge and experience. A good memory also helps considerably. Since the total production of the Wedgwood firm over the past 200 years has been enormous and records of what has been produced were far from complete, there is always the possibility that a collector can find something that exists nowhere else in the world. There have been one-of-a-kind experimental pieces or limited runs of plates, urns and other items where all but a few have been broken or have otherwise disappeared. Many sets of dishes have been decorated to order for a particular family and presentation pieces made to commemorate important historical occasions. These are true collector's items and are always the envy of every other Wedgwood collector.

The problem of where to find old Wedgwood can be answered in a hundred different ways by as many experienced collectors. Most veteran collectors will not answer that question at all, for they have their favourite sources and are quite secretive about them. Where one is able to purchase Wedgwood for his collection will depend upon several factors. If a collector has more time than money, he can sometimes make excellent purchases at bona-fide estate auctions, for if he attends enough of these, in England or America, it is a sure bet that a worthwhile piece of Wedgwood

Creamware plate with a message, printed and hand-painted in colours with green predominating. Marked: Wedgwood, Etruria, England, 1871. [Klamkin]

Creamware commemorative plate, 'Old Ironsides'. Printed decoration. Diameter, 10in. [Klamkin]

will be sold sometime. When it is not blue and white jasperware or an extremely important item such as a Portland vase copy or a Flaxman plaque, often there will be no one attending the auction as knowledgeable as the dedicated Wedgwood collector. The housewife who buys antiques at auctions because they are pretty and the shopowner who deals in a general line of antiques will only bid so high on Wedgwood if they are not certain it is really old or important. Since the study of Wedgwood is so involved, the average antique dealer is usually not too knowledgeable; there are too many other things that he has to know about. That is why there are dealers who specialise only in Wedgwood. The specialists must purchase Wedgwood in large amounts in order to satisfy their many collectors and cannot usually afford to spend an entire day attending an auction unless a large amount of Wedgwood has been advertised. Often, there is no way that the Wedgwood dealer can know about local estate auctions. There are too many of them and unless they are important enough to have been advertised nationally, they are of no interest to him.

Here are some examples of Wedgwood bought by collectors at estate auctions recently and where the specialised knowledge of the collector came in handy. One collector attended a large, nationally advertised estate auction where he recognised a complete dessert set of moonlight lustre in shell shapes, including six-footed nautilus-shaped compotes. The bottom of each piece had the impressed mark 'WEDGWOOD' and the collector was certain that the set would bring a very high price because the occasion of the auction was the dispersal for the heirs of the possessions of a noted collector of antiques, and was widely advertised and attended by important dealers in antiques. However, the collector overheard two representatives of one of the largest antiques dealers discussing the set and their conclusion was that Wedgwood never made any of those 'pink dishes' and that they must be phony or not old enough to bother about. The collector bought the entire set cheaply, his special knowedge of Wedgwood giving him a distinct advantage over experts with a general knowledge of antiques. The Wedgwood student knows and recognises a nautilus dessert service as an adaptation in pottery of Josiah Wedgwood's interest in conchology.

Creamware, 'The Federal Bowl', made for Martin's Store in Washington, DC in limited edition. Drawings of official seals of original thirteen states and Great Seal of the United States were made by Alan Price. On inside of bowl is copy of Savage's painting, 'Washington's Family'. Portraits of Washington, Jefferson, Jackson and Lincoln adorn sides of bowl. Diameter, 10in. [Jo-Anne Blum, Inc]

(left) Creamware urn with surface agate glaze. Gilded festoons and handles. Marked: Wedgwood and Bentley. C1772. Height, 12in. [Schaffer Collection]; (right) Creamware clock. Hand-painted in pastel colours and gold lustre. Finial is world globe. Marked: Wedgwood. C1860. Height, 11¾. [Jo-Anne Blum, Inc]

Another instance where the specialised knowledge in the field of Wedgwood collecting is advantageous can be illustrated by citing another auction. This was a small local estate auction held in a small town in New England; there was little of importance in the inventory and there was no Wedgwood advertised. The auctioneer is an authority on early American antiques and is quite knowledgeable in the general field of furniture and glassware. Each item he sells is described as honestly and accurately as possible. During the sale he held up an octagonal shaped bowl in an orange lustre glaze and asked for an opening bid. He described the bowl as being very 'unusual', for it was marked 'Wedgwood' but didn't look like any Wedgwood that he had ever seen. He suggested that it might have been an 'experimental' piece. The Wedgwood collector attending that auction bought a fairyland lustre bowl for one-twentieth of the current market price, making the time spent at one otherwise uninteresting auction well worthwhile. Fairyland lustre is not an item that most experts on antiques would recognise as having unusual value, it is not even antique, but every Wedgwood collector would be delighted to own an example of Wedgwood in the art pottery style of the beginning of this century.

Where else besides auctions does one find Wedgwood for a collection? Again, we are still discussing the fairly new collector, who has more time than money to spend

26

but is still hunting for the unusual and the interesting. Visit as many antique shops as you have the time for. Look through each dealer's stock, even though he might specialise in a type of antique entirely different from Wedgwood. A fine jasper dip acanthus bowl was bought from a dealer who specialises in Tiffany and other glass-ware and ceramics of the art nouveau period. Do not be afraid to tell a dealer that you are a Wedgwood collector. He may have tucked away one piece of Wedgwood that will make the visit worth his time and yours. Often a dealer will know some other Wedgwood collector willing to show you what he has and perhaps sell a duplicate. Often, too, a dealer will take the name of a collector in case he finds an interesting lot of Wedgwood or even one interesting piece in the future. The collector is under no obligation to buy something he has been called in to see, but it is a courtesy to look at the item. Often antique dealers have sources that are not available to the collector.

The above suggestions are time-consuming. Sometimes a first-rate piece of antique Wedgwood is found at an auction, but the really important pieces are more usually bought from the few dealers who are Wedgwood specialists. New York, Chicago, London, and Philadelphia are perhaps the most promising cities for the Wedgwood collector. However, the dozen or so dealers who do specialise in old Wedgwood usually advertise nationally in hobby, antiques and collectors' magazines in England and America. Apart from museums and private collections, the largest and most

(left) *Creamware candle-vase. Lid reverses to hold candle. Marked: Wedgwood (impressed). C1775. Height, 6¼in [Klamkin];* (right) *Green jasper chessman (pawn). Marked: Wedgwood (accompanied by a 'v'). Chessmen were designed by Flaxman in 1784. Height, 4in. [Mattatuck Museum]*

varied amounts of choice Wedgwood are in the inventories of these dealers. It does not usually stay there long, nor do the dealers worry when it does. Each year every good piece of old Wedgwood increases in value and eventually the right collector comes along for everything. The dealer's largest problem is continually adding to his supply of Wedgwood in order to keep his collectors happy. The experienced Wedgwood collector has his favourite dealer, just as each dealer has his list of collectors and a note of what each collector wants. Many dealers began as collectors themselves.

The dealers keep a mailing list of Wedgwood collectors in a large geographical area and inform them regularly of their acquisitions. Many Wedgwood dealers and their clients have become good friends. The common interest in Wedgwood and the mutual benefits to be gained from such a friendship are advantageous to both parties. As long as the collector agrees that the dealer is entitled to his profit, this kind of mutually beneficial relationship can be, and often is, the basis for some of the finest private Wedgwood collections in the world. This fact, that the most important pieces of antique Wedgwood are often sold before the average collector ever gets an opportunity to see them, should not discourage the young collector or those with limited funds. As one's collection grows, if it has been bought wisely, it also grows in importance and increases in value. The dealers recognise this and are

Basalt vases in two sizes. Enamel decoration. Both marked: Wedgwood. Heights, 9in and 4in. [Jo-Anne Blum, Inc]

28

(left) *Basalt vase with gold slip decoration. Marked: Wedgwood. Late nineteenth century. Height, 13in. [Jo-Anne Blum, Inc]; (right) Miniature basalt bust. Subject: Mark Antony. Marked: Wedgwood. C1780. Height, 4in. [Spero Collection]*

willing to call those collectors who might not be their most important and profitable customers at present, but who, with time, will become a market for larger amounts and more important pieces of ceramics. Or, better still for the dealer, a small collection which over the years he has helped increase might be put back on the market and could conceivably be offered to him first. The dealer is constantly looking for sources to buy as well as sell.

The collector of antiques in any field should also be aware that the dealers are constantly active in buying and selling to each other. At most important antique shows there often is more trading done among the dealers before the show is opened to the public than is done during the actual show. In this way, the Wedgwood or Tiffany or antique jewellery specialist is able to keep the market prices for his particular speciality fairly constant. Other dealers in antiques are a constant source of supply to the Wedgwood specialist. Nevertheless, the collector of limited means can still find an occasional 'bargain' in old or scarce Wedgwood. One cannot easily gather an important collection by buying from sources other than specialist dealers in a short period of time, but it is possible to satisfy the collector's acquisitive nature by employing a lot of time and patience, and, most particularly, knowledge.

29

(left) White smear-glaze pitcher, embossed neo-gothic design. Marked: Wedgwood. Probably mid-nineteenth century. Height (without handle), 3⅛in. [Klamkin]; (right) Bone-china compote. Shell and coral shape. Hand-gilded borders and trim. Marked: Wedgwood (outline of Portland Vase). Late nineteenth century. Height, 9in. [Spero Collection]

Almost 100 years ago, Eliza Meteyard, writing on the subject of Wedgwood collecting, pointed out that the dealers and their agents had been scouring the countryside of England and had stripped it clean of good specimens of what was then 'antique Wedgwood'. This is a process that is still continuing, though today not only British dealers but Americans, too, track down every good piece of purchasable old Wedgwood like detectives. Although this practice is continuous, there is always some good old Wedgwood to be found in England and many other parts of Europe every year. One reason is that much of the Wedgwood that was 'antique' to Eliza Meteyard in 1875 is now in museums, but since Miss Meteyard's excellent book was written there have been types of Wedgwood made which are as much collector's items as the original Flaxman plaques and vases were in her day.

For those collectors who are fortunate enough to be able to travel, the search for Wedgwood can take place almost anywhere in the world. So much of it has been made and the market has always been an international one, even from Josiah Wedgwood's day. Eighteenth-century Wedgwood was shipped to the Netherlands, Italy, France, Germany and Russia as well as everywhere in the United Kingdom. Wedgwood, who was in sympathy with the American Revolution, had a large and ready market in America before and after that war. Those states that were settled at that time used quantities of Queen's ware and with the prosperity that came after the Revolution, the decorative wares were bought also. Since most Wedgwood

30

is aesthetically appealing, the decorative wares were often kept by heirs where other examples of early pottery were carelessly treated or disposed of. In many cases, where an early piece of Wedgwood was broken at some time, expense and effort were not spared in making the necessary repairs. There are many pieces of truly old Wedgwood that have truly old repairs.

The really dedicated collector of old Wedgwood may find what he seeks just about everywhere and often in the most surprising places. If the collector has neither the time nor the patience, he will do well to acquaint himself with a dealer who specialises in Wedgwood. Dealers who exhibit at major antique shows and fairs in America and England can be visited and the matter discussed. Many important dealers travel long distances with their collections if an antique show is large enough or if they know that some of their important collectors live near the city where the antique show is being held. A large part of the dealer's business is done at antique shows, since not only established collectors of Wedgwood are customers, but lovers of fine antiques and interior designers attend as well. Many dealers sell only at these shows.

A word of warning to the new collector: do not be over cautious about purchasing anything that will be a welcome addition to your collection, providing the price is right and you really like it. It might not be there tomorrow. 'I wish I had bought it!' is a frequently heard lament at many Wedgwood Society meetings.

Cup and saucer of caneware. Hand-painted with blue enamel in bamboo motif. Interior of cup glazed. Marked: Wedgwood. C1790. Diameter of cup, 3in. [Spero Collection]

5
Wedgwood Ware

CREAMWARE OR QUEEN'S WARE

When Josiah Wedgwood started his own business in 1759 at the Ivy House Works, conditions were primitive for the potters of that area, though clay for potting and wood for fuel, the two necessary raw materials for the potter, were readily available. Josiah's first achievement was his invention of a green glaze. Tortoiseshell and agate ware were already being made and Wedgwood was aware of the market for those products. Salt glaze ware, which Wedgwood probably had made in partnership with Thomas Whieldon, was no longer in demand. Imitation fruit and vegetable shapes in the green glaze were made to compete with the imported porcelain of the

Creamware tureen and covered pitcher with blue hand-painted decoration. Note twisted handle on pitcher. Both pieces marked. C1775. Length of tureen, 8in. [Schaffer Collection]

Tureen, creamware, with underdish and cover. Marked: Wedgwood (impressed). Shape ≠ 1 in 1774 catalogue. Hand-painted border in green and mulberry. Height, 12in. Length, 16in. [Klamkin]

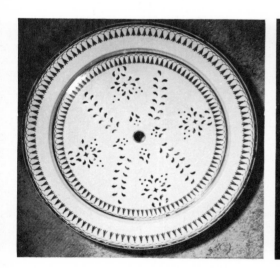

(left) *Round meat platter with strainer. Diameter, 18¼in. [Klamkin]; (right) Wedgwood's creamware plates were made to stack and nest. Stack of soup-plates demonstrates the precision with which eighteenth-century plates were made. This feature facilitated packing and shipping as well as storage. Width, 9¾in. All marked. [Klamkin].*

Three-tiered pierced cheese mould. C1790. Height, 4½in. [Schaffer Collection]

rococo period of the middle eighteenth century. The leaf-shaped dishes and cauli-flower ware of the early period are difficult to find today except in the collections of fine museums. The green glaze has been made fairly consistently throughout the history of the firm and has always found a ready market.

In 1762 Wedgwood moved from the Ivy House Works to the Brick House or Bell Works, so called because workmen were called to work by the ringing of a bell rather than the blowing of a horn (which had been the custom elsewhere). By 1763, Josiah Wedgwood, after several years of experiment, perfected a 'species of earthen-ware for the table, quite new in appearance, covered with a rich and brilliant glaze, bearing sudden alterations of heat and cold, manufactured with ease and expedition and consequently cheap'. This new ware changed the eating habits of people every-where in the western world.

Creamware is considered by historians of ceramics to be Wedgwood's greatest accomplishment, though he did not invent this light-coloured clay body, which many potters in the Staffordshire region of England made long before and during his time. Competition from the Chinese porcelains that had been imported for many years before the development of creamware inspired British potters to create a less ex-pensive table ware. Wedgwood's refinement of creamware accomplished this pur-pose, and since it could be sold for a much lower price than the imported porcelain, it soon became widely used and, therefore, fashionable.

Wedgwood's early creamware differs from that of his competitors in that he in-troduced the use of Cornwall clay, creating a lighter stronger body with a more uniform texture. His glazes were fine and even and the shapes used were probably the best designs for dinner ware ever made. The colour varied according to the mix-ture of clay used and ranged from a deep saffron to an extremely light cream. Most

34

of the early creamware was for table use, but many ornamental pieces were made as well. Centrepieces, baskets, vases, statuettes and plaques are some of the early creamware items that are now rare and highly collectable.

Before the development of creamware, only the wealthy could afford dishes of any quality at all. Wooden trenchers, highly unhygienic, and coarse earthenware were commonly used for serving and as plates from which to eat. Some of the more fortunate owned a supply of tinware or pewter. Josiah Wedgwood, by marketing his creamware at a reasonable price, made it possible for people to own sets of well designed and beautiful dishes. While Wedgwood was not alone in producing good quality creamware, his was by far the best produced in his time and the most durable. He was astute enough both to mark his dishes and to market them intelligently.

In 1762 Josiah Wedgwood supplied a breakfast service for Queen Charlotte, wife of George III, and thereafter creamware was marketed as 'Queen's ware' and Josiah was allowed to call himself 'Potter to the Queen'. Wedgwood's Queen's ware was produced in enormous quantities and marketed everywhere in the world where the British traded. Hundreds of shapes were designed and Queen's ware dishes were made for any purpose that could be thought of. Sets of dishes were made to order with coats-of-arms, special border designs and monograms. Undecorated plates were sent to foreign countries where local artists decorated them to their own tastes. Great care was taken that the design for each shape of dish was as functional as possible as well as graceful and attractive.

There are two major aspects of Wedgwood's creamware that make it unique. The first is the quality of the body and glaze and the second is the design, so perfect that many of these early shapes have yet to be improved upon. Cornwall clay, a variety of kaolin, mixed with flint, was used for the glaze on Queen's ware so that,

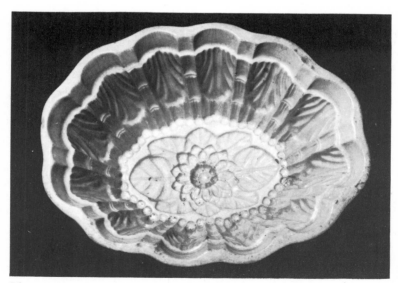

Blancmange mould, Creamware. Close-up view shows careful moulding of inverted design. 1882. Marked: Wedgwood. Height, 4in. Length, 7¼in. [Klamkin]

35

(left) *Creamware urn with chocolate brown slip. Marked: Wedgwood. Eighteenth century. Height, 10½in. [Schaffer Collection]; (right) Creamware candlesticks. Hand-painted border in green and brown. Shape 34 in 1774 catalogue. Marked: Wedgwood (impressed). C1800. Height, 7¼in. [Klamkin]*

when fired, the glaze and body of a plate became one and were not apt to craze, a fault which one finds with many of the light clay bodies of other potters of the period. Lead poisoning, a hazard common in the potteries of early times, was avoided by Wedgwood by a sharp reduction of that material in his creamware.

The texture of the clay used made it possible for dishes of light weight to be designed—both an aesthetic and a commercial advantage. Transportation in Josiah Wedgwood's day was extremely primitive and the lighter the ware, the more could be transported. Because the Queen's ware, after firing, was extremely strong, it was less apt to arrive at its destination in pieces than were the wares of Wedgwood's competitors.

Wedgwood never ceased designing shapes for his Queen's ware body that were unique and useful. The teapots were comfortable to hold; the spouts did not drip, nor did the covers fall off while tea was being poured. Meat platters were designed so that the juice drained off and the slabs of meat did not sit in their own juice. While drains for meat platters were not invented by Wedgwood, the pierced work on his drains is done more artistically and deftly than on the Chinese export porcelain of the same era.

Designs for tureens, sauce boats, plates for every conceivable course, condiment sets, centrepieces and tea-sets were all given equal care and thought and many of these same designs are still being used for modern Wedgwood production. Eighteenth-century dinner plates and soup plates stack more uniformly than many of the modern and so-called functional sets designed today. Indeed, the shapes of Wedgwood's early Queen's ware were so perfect that many collectors desire the undecorated pieces.

While much of the eighteenth-century Queen's ware was undecorated, many sets of dishes were decorated by hand with tasteful border patterns and others were transfer-printed. Often we find a combination of both the transfer-printing and hand-decoration on the same plate, a technique that is sometimes used at the factory today. The early transfer designs were executed in Liverpool by the firm of Sadler & Green, who held the patent for this kind of work. Wedgwood employed his own artists to hand-decorate his Queen's ware. He sometimes sent plates to ladies living near his factory who were adept with the paintbrush. In most cases, the border designs and free-hand painting are done with discretion and taste, most of the decoration being simple and subdued.

The varied borders listed in Wedgwood's first pattern book for use in decorating Queen's ware consist of designs of leaves, flowers, shells, Etruscan motifs, ivy sprigs, birds, calico patterns and many others, each being executed in combinations of colours that are pleasing and reserved. Often the more simple borders were combined in the design. Many of the original border patterns have been revived by the factory at various times, for they are difficult to surpass.

Wedgwood did his best to design articles for his Queen's ware to satisfy every possible market. Baby feeders, pans for use in the dairy, moulds for jellies, pots, scales, candlesticks and food warmers are only a few of the useful items that were made and marketed along with dinner-sets and tea-sets. He also made tiles for dairies in quantity. Every piece of eighteenth-century Queen's ware was made with care and each is a work of art. As much effort was employed to find the best possible design for a curd pot as was given to a soup tureen.

Creamware twig basket and woven pattern embossed plate. Basket shape has been popular since eighteenth century. Both marked: Wedgwood. Basket, 1913. Length of basket, 8in. Diameter of plate, 9½in. [Klamkin]

(above) *Cup and saucer in Creamware. Printed designs of gardening tools and spinning tools in shades of brown. Hand-lined. Marked: Wedgwood. Eighteenth century. Height of cup, 2½in.* [Klamkin]

Creamware plate. One of second set of series of twelve with engravings by Clare Leighton for 'New England Industries'. Also a reverse of plate showing mark and legend. Diameter, 10in. [Leighton]

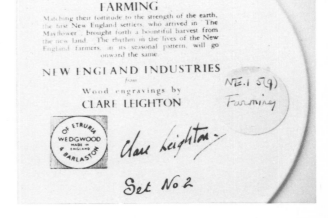

FARMING

Matching their fortitude to the strength of the earth, the first New England settlers, who arrived in 'The Mayflower', brought forth a bountiful harvest from the new land. The rhythm in the lives of the New England farmers, in its seasonal pattern, will go onward the same.

NEW ENGLAND INDUSTRIES
from
Wood engravings by
CLARE LEIGHTON

OF ETRURIA
WEDGWOOD
MADE IN
ENGLAND
& BARLASTON

Clare Leighton

NE.1 5(9)
Farming

Set No 2

(left) *Creamware plate, printed in black. 'American Sailing Ship' series. Diameter, 10in. [Klamkin];* (right) *Creamware plate, showing St Clement Danes Church, Strand, London—one of series of twelve different designs made by Wedgwood during World War II to raise money for British War Relief. Diameter, 10in. [Coe Collection]*

Examples of eighteenth-century Queen's ware can be seen in many museums. The collector should remember, however, that the same shapes and border patterns were used over and over again by the factory and, therefore, the fact that a piece of Queen's ware resembles another in a photograph or in a museum does not automatically date it to the eighteenth century. Other criteria must be taken into consideration when identifying a piece of Queen's ware to Josiah Wedgwood's period of production. The quality of the body and glaze, the border pattern or other decoration and the mark are all identifying features with which the collector should become familiar. Remember that some of the eighteenth-century Wedgwood was exported for decoration in the country for which it was intended, so there is still some early Queen's ware to be found with decoration unlike that which Wedgwood used.

The largest, most elaborate pieces of Queen's ware are the most sought after: the pierced meat platters, the majestic tureens, the chestnut dishes and the condiment sets, almost never found complete. The decorative items made in the eighteenth century are also highly collectable. Early vases, flower and bough pots are desired by all collectors of eighteenth-century Wedgwood. The creamware that was decorated to alter its appearance—moonlight lustre, agate ware and silver resist—deserve space of their own and will be discussed later. There were some early creamware plaques made by Wedgwood and decorated by George Stubbs, who specialised in painting horses, but very few of these have ever shown up in recent times. One was sold at auction recently in London for the sum of £10,000 ($24,000), a category of collecting which is hardly within the reach of the average collector.

Josiah Wedgwood's Queen's ware was the single most important accomplishment in the history of pottery in the past 200 years. It is, perhaps, the very quality of appearing so modern that has kept the unaware antique collector from buying all he could find.

VARIEGATED WARES

Technically, both variegated and lustre ware made by Wedgwood belong to the category of Queen's ware. However, they are both so different in appearance that they might confuse a collector who is not familiar with the alterations Wedgwood made to his creamware body in order to change its original appearance.

His first attempts to imitate porphyry were done by applying to his creamware a coloured glaze made by mixing various colours so as to give a slight resemblance to stone. Although he later improved upon this method by mixing various coloured clays so that the body of a vase was coloured throughout, he used the first method to decorate overstock creamware. We often see marbleised plinths and bases that were made by the first method.

The later vases of the variegated wares are far superior artistically and are very rare, beyond the price of the average collector today. These 'pebble vases' were made in a great variety of colours, and as imitations of various kinds of stones are highly successful. Serpentine, agate, verde antique, green jasper, grey granite, and red porphyry are the stones listed in Eliza Meteyard's 'Handbook' as those which Wedgwood imitated. Most of the variegated ware was made in the classic shapes of the jasperware urns and vases. The decorations used were often festoons, wreaths and husks. Usually the glaze is highly polished and very smooth and has no tendency to craze. Any piece of this early variegated ware is worth buying.

Moonlight lustre potpourri jar. Top has holes for scent while inner cover keeps potpourri fresh. Pink shaded and mottled glaze. Marked: Wedgwood (impressed). Early nineteenth century. Height, 14in. [Jo-Anne Blum, Inc]

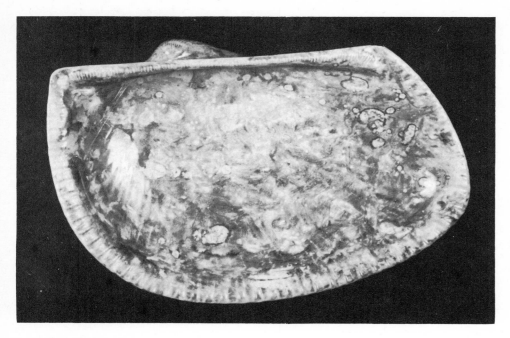

Moonlight lustre shell, early nineteenth century. Lustre glaze shades from pink to purple and has flecks of gold. Length, 11½in. [Schaffer Collection]

LUSTREWARES

Another glaze which altered the appearance of Josiah Wedgwood's creamware completely is moonlight lustre. This process involved the mixture of colour pigments that gave a lustre effect. The work was not entirely successful in Josiah I's day and most of the marked lustre seen today is from the early nineteenth century. It was used largely on pearlware and made in shell shapes. The iridescent effect is ideal for the nautilus shape and dessert sets were very successful when made of this ware.

Early creamware vases were often decorated with gilding, enamelling and bas relief of another colour, while many other Queen's ware vases were left undecorated. While large quantities of variegated and otherwise decorated creamware vases were made, not too many have survived. This is unfortunate, because they are a highly successful design to the modern eye.

PEARLWARE

Wedgwood's pearlware is essentially made from the same clay body as Queen's ware. The addition of cobalt to the mixture of clay negates the cream colour when the ware is fired. Pearlware, made to satisfy a market that demanded whiter dishes and to compete with the bone china of the late eighteenth century, is still available in some quantity and only recently has become quite collectable.

Pearlware covered casserole dish. Fish-shaped finial on cover. Blue and red printed border decorations. Marked: Vieux Rouen, Wedgwood, Etruria, England, Importe D'Angleterre, U.S.A. Patent, June 21st 1910. Diameter, 9in. [Klamkin]

Pearlware game-pie dish. Rabbit finial. Flow-blue under-glaze decoration. Marked: Wedgwood. C1875. Length, 8½in. Height, 6½in. [Klamkin]

Wedgwood first made pearlware in 1779 and its production continued throughout most of the nineteenth century. While it is technically earthenware rather than china, its production seemed to satisfy the demand for a white clay body until the Wedgwood factory began its second period of bone-china production at the end of the nineteenth century, when there was no longer any need for pearlware. It has not been produced in any quantity in the present century.

Early pearlware can be identified by the white appearance of the undecorated part of a plate; and where the glaze is thick, round the base of the dish, for instance, by a blueish cast. Some of the most typically Victorian items made by the Wedgwood potters consisted of pearlware, some of which was hand-painted or decorated with transfer patterns. Between 1840 and 1868 the word 'Pearl' was often marked on the underside of plates to identify the ware and later the letter 'P' was used. The name of the pattern was often printed on the undersides of dinner-sets along with the impressed 'Wedgwood'.

One of the reasons for the neglect of pearlware was that the early collectors thought creamware to be more elegant and attractive. Therefore, the early books about collecting have largely ignored pearlware or spoken about it with a certain amount of disdain. As time has passed, however, it has become obvious that pearlware is as important artistically in the story of Wedgwood as any other clay body or glaze. Now that the Victorian styles of decoration are so far removed, it is possible for us to see what was of enduring artistic importance in that period. Although it was invented in the eighteenth century, pearlware was produced in large quantities in the nineteenth century, and in each category of earthenware produced since then, the outstanding examples continue to be Wedgwood.

Flow blue, a type of decoration held in high esteem by collectors of primitive and useful wares, is always more appealing when it is marked 'Wedgwood'. Its transfer patterns are usually laid on with more precision and the clay shapes that they decor— ate are usually a little more refined. Much of it was made for the American market and there is still enough of it around for the American collector to specialise in it without too large an investment.

The greatest problem in collecting old pearlware is recognising it. It was made throughout the nineteenth century to compete with other contemporary china and pottery, and looks very much like other wares made in Staffordshire at the same

(left) Pearlware ladle. Blue printed design in bowl and on handle. Marked: Wedg-wood. 1890. Diameter of bowl, 3¾in. [Klamkin]; (right) Pearlware slop jar. Blue transfer-printed under-glaze. Marked: Wedgwood. Diamond-shaped lozenge reg-istry mark sets date at 1879. Height, 12in. [Klamkin]

(above) *Pearlware bowl. 'Indian Pattern' printed in underglaze blue with gold lustre hand-applied decoration. Dragon-shape handles. Marked: Wedgwood. 1878. Diameter, 11in. [Klamkin]; (left) Pearlware plate made for British market. Printed with over-glaze hand-enamelled decoration. Marked: Wedgwood, Etruria, England. C1905. Diameter, 10in. [Klamkin]*

time. Some pearlware cannot be easily distinguished from Chinese export porcelain of the eighteenth century.

When in doubt, simply turn it over and look for the mark on the underside. If it is Wedgwood, it will say so. Unfortunately, little has been written about pearlware and the neophyte collector is apt to exclaim, 'I didn't know Wedgwood made that!' But do not be afraid to invest in it. It is still inexpensive; and with more knowledge at your disposal than the average antique dealer, you may be able to find some of the really old pieces. In any case, little pearlware was made during this century, so those pieces that are not really antique will soon become so. Remember that the addition of three letters or a number and two letters to the name (see Appendix on marks) will enable you to date your piece to the month and year of manufacture.

Odd dishes in pearlware can be useful to you as serving pieces; most of them will cost no more than good new china and many of the border and all-over patterns are beautiful. The larger useful pieces, resembling what is generally thought of as iron-stone, are handy as plant containers; and some of these have designs and patterns that are quite formal and attractive. The cache pots, pitchers and washbowls popular now are worth much more than most old pottery if they are marked 'Wedgwood'. The old decorated washbowls are extremely attractive and functional salad bowls. For those who like the old cobalt blue border patterns, Wedgwood pearlware is ideal to collect. The blue transfers took better on its white ground than on Queen's ware, and there are many useful pieces wth cobalt borders.

ROSSO ANTICO

Redware, made from Staffordshire clay coloured with iron oxide, was made in that region long before Josiah Wedgwood became a master potter. Because it had been used for common wares, Josiah Wedgwood disapproved of its use for his decorative items, and it was not until 1765 that he used the red clay with success. Then the revival in interest in the antiquities of Egypt led him to design canopic vases, sphinxes and other ornamental objects with Egyptian motifs; and he often used a ground of red clay with a black basalt applied design. Later, in 1789, he made basalt ware with red applied ornament, which met with greater commercial success.

Wedgwood called his redware 'rosso antico' in order to promote it as something different from the common red clay pottery. It was more successful than he had anticipated, and though he gave it less attention than he did to the experimentation

(left to right) *Rosso antico vase with black bas relief; basalt vase with relief in Egyptian motifs in rosso antico; rosso antico pitcher with black relief. All marked: Wedgwood. Height of largest vase, 8in. [Spero Collection]*

and design of jasperware and basalt, the examples that remain are artistically successful.

Rosso antico ranged in colour from a light red to a chocolate-brown. Wedgwood used this clay body for vases decorated with encaustic designs in the Greek style. Josiah Wedgwood II used a rosso antico body at the beginning of the nineteenth century that was lighter in colour than his father's earlier redware, and decorated it in enamel in the Chinese manner popular at the time. Similar ware in basalt was also made then. The enamelled redware style was revived again in the middle of the nineteenth century, but the quality of the enamelling did not compare with the earlier work.

Another revival of the red clay body took place in 1920 with the Wedgwood firm's 'Capri ware', and it, too, was made in shapes adapted from Chinese porcelain. This ware is now being collected and has risen rather rapidly in value.

CANEWARE

Cane-coloured ware, made during the first Wedgwood period, was used for many decorative items, and is well worth collecting. It was highly adaptable to the silver shapes used by many of the Staffordshire potters and a good many items were made for the tea table.

Bamboo ware, another name for this type of pottery, could be used to make pots for which basalt and jasper were unsuitable. Planters and bulb pots in the shape of bamboo sticks, fine engine-turned bowls and dishes, and, later, game-pie dishes were

(left) *Caneware spill vase. Blue relief. Smear-glazed. C1810. Marked: Wedgwood. Height, 3½in. [Klamkin]; (right) Caneware honey pot in shape of beehive. Smear-glazed. Marked: Wedgwood. C1815. Height, 4¼in. [Klamkin]*

Caneware game-pie dish with 'cauliflower' finial. Marked: Wedgwood. C1810. Length, 9in. Height to finial, 6in. [Jo-Anne Blum, Inc]

made of both glazed and unglazed caneware. Early caneware was often decorated with enamel or embossed relief patterns.

Pastry ware, made to resemble crust, was made from caneware during the flour famine of the Napoleonic Wars. These pieces, really casserole dishes, were highly successful commercially and were made during several periods in the nineteenth century. Many of the same moulds were used later in the century for majolica casseroles.

DRABWARE

Drabware was invented by the second Josiah Wedgwood. The fired clay is olive–grey in colour and items made of it are scarce today. It was used in both smear-glaze and unglazed states, the former having an extremely hard and brittle appearance. Items in drabware were often decorated with bas relief in lavender, white, blue, or, sometimes, brown motifs. The item most often seen today is a smear-glaze teapot with a spaniel finial on the cover. This shape evidently was popular because it is often seen in white smear-glaze also. It was made in several sizes.

(above) *Drabware teapot, smear-glazed. Spaniel finial on cover. Spout damaged. Marked: Wedgwood. Height, 4½in. [Klamkin]*
(right) *White stoneware trembleuse. This covered cup was made throughout the nineteenth century. Marked: Wedgwood. Height, 4½in. [Klamkin]*

WHITEWARE

Whiteware was also a product of the early nineteenth century. It was modelled into simple yet classic designs for cups with a highly polished interior glaze, and also used for other shapes. This was a period when hand-decorated china began to flood the market and whiteware was produced undecorated for amateur decorators. It was also, of course, decorated at the factory, somewhat more successfully than the amateur-painted examples that have survived. Coloured bas relief was often applied to the white body. It was made both glazed and unglazed; the glazed ware closely resembles earlier examples of salt glaze, but it is, technically, a smear glaze. Salt glaze, made by many Staffordshire potters, has a more pitted surface than the smear glaze made by Wedgwood.

While the above-mentioned stoneware bodies are often classified as 'ornamental', there are always doubts whether many of the objects are not, in fact, useful. Just as there were 'useful' objects made in the 'ornamental' bodies of jasper and basalt, there were many ornamental objects made in what is arbitrarily considered to be a useful body, such as Wedgwood's Queen's ware. Classification depends on what the body was designed to do. Jasper, basalt, rosso antico, caneware, drabware and white-ware were all developed mainly for decorative items.

BASALT

The partnership of Josiah Wedgwood and Thomas Bentley, proposed in 1766 and formalised in 1769, did not involve Wedgwood's Queen's ware production, nor any of the so-called 'useful wares'. The purpose of the partnership was to develop, make and market decorative wares, which included articles made of a black clay body that resembled bronze when polished. This smooth-grained pottery derived its colouring from iron oxide, which is found in water drained from the coalmines. Clay containing such water produced a body that Wedgwood found suitable for busts and other ornamental pieces of pottery. Of all the clay bodies he developed and made, basalt has been the one most consistently in demand.

While Josiah Wedgwood did not invent the basalt clay, he refined it highly through lengthy experimentation, and eventually was able to produce a hard black matte finish for his Etruscan vases, which had enormous commercial success during the neo-classic period. Successful production of basalt items dates from the beginning of the Wedgwood and Bentley partnership. Any items that could possibly be made in this popular ware were produced in large quantities. Engine turning (see Glossary) was used for vase decoration—and on bowls, cache pots, glaciers, cups and other

Basalt tablet. Subject: A Bacchanalian Sacrifice. Marked: Wedgwood (three times). 1769. 20¼in x 8¾in. [Jo-Anne Blum, Inc]

49

(left) *Basalt bust of Mercury. Originally modelled by Flaxman, this bust has always been popular and has been produced often. Height, 20in. [Jo-Anne Blum, Inc];* (right) *Basalt squirrel has amber glass eyes set in. The design by Mr Light, art master of Hanley School, seems to have been adapted from an early Bow figure. Marked: Wedgwood. 1912. Height, 5½in. [Klamkin]*

receptacles. Basalt ware was decorated with bas relief, encaustic figures painted in the Greek manner, enamel or left plain. There was more basalt produced during this early period than jasper.

Basalt, because of the density of its composition, became an ideal material from which to model intaglios, busts, and portrait medallions. Historical and mythological figures and faces were turned out in great numbers and the public's acceptance was gratifying and immediate. Basalt has been produced continuously since it was first developed, with the exception of a period during World War II.

To the Wedgwood collector, the discovery of a piece of basalt, no matter how small, marked 'Wedgwood and Bentley' is an exciting find; for the workmanship in any of the early basalt ware is gem-like, of excellent quality. Basalt was made in a flat finish or a highly polished shiny finish, and many of the early vases and busts were bronzed or gilded. Over the years basalt develops a patina that is satiny in appearance and feel.

The details of even the smallest portrait intaglios are amazingly life-like and many of the portraits are recognisable as important dignitaries of Wedgwood's day. Characters from mythology, Egyptians, Greeks and Romans, animals, birds and great religious figures were the subjects of many of these cameos and intaglios. The intaglios, tiny inside-out portraits, were used for personalised seals, as decorations on chatelaines and as gems in rings and other jewellery.

Wedgwood also made larger intaglios, which were meant to be displayed in sets in lined drawers of cabinets, the basalt against white lining and jasper cameos against contrasting colours. Intaglios were made to be collected. Once plentiful, they are now difficult to find and expensive, the more so if the portraits can be identified as historically important figures. Small basalt medallions and intaglios are often made into rings, pins and tiepins today. Wedgwood's basalt is gem-like in strength and will not crack or chip easily.

The price of Wedgwood and Bentley basalt ware is extremely high. Early basalt has become very rare, and nineteenth-century basalt is in great demand among collectors. There have been some exceptionally good designs made in basalt in this century that are very collectable also: the engine-turned bowls designed and signed by Keith Murray are well worth owning; and the award-winning demitasse set in simple unpolished black is a modern item that will probably increase in value. The design of the latter is typical of our own time and the simple profile of the coffee pot is striking.

Wedgwood's finest accomplishments in basalt ware were, of course, the large tablets, the busts designed by Flaxman, or Hoskins and Grant, and the magnificent vases and urns designed in the classic manner. For the antique buff or the modernist, there is much satisfaction in owning Wedgwood basalt. There is something very solid and masculine about its appearance.

(below) *Basalt plaque. Subject: The Frightened Horse. Modelled by George Stubbs. Marked: Wedgwood. C1780. Length, 6in. [Spero Collection];* (right) *Basalt glacier showing interior insert, which is perforated and fixed at bottom centre. Top rim is removable. Engine-turned surface and moulded relief. Marked: Wedgwood. Diameter, 8½in. [Mattatuck Museum]*

JASPERWARE

Josiah Wedgwood and Thomas Bentley became partners for the purpose of producing decorative wares in the style of the Greek and Roman classical designs. Shortly after the partnership was established, they bought land outside Burslem and built a factory (and homes for workers) which they called Etruria. The useful wares were still being made at the old Bell Works and until 1773–4 the two kinds of production were kept separate. After that time all operations were moved to Etruria, which produced all the Wedgwood until 1940 when the present factory was built in Barlaston.

Wedgwood's first classical designs were made in the basalt body, but after two years of experimenting with various clays he was able in 1776 to produce a new stoneware—the first jasperware. It was white with a dense opaque waxen body very much like basalt in quality and hardness. Wedgwood also made a semi-opaque biscuit, whiter than the first, which sometimes had a faint blueish tint due to the addition of sulphate of baryta. The waxen-like density of the white body and the hardness seem to have been secrets that died with Josiah I. No jasper made since is of quite the same quality.

Once the white jasper bodies were perfected, Wedgwood experimented with colouring the clay so that he could reproduce the bas reliefs made in glass and stone

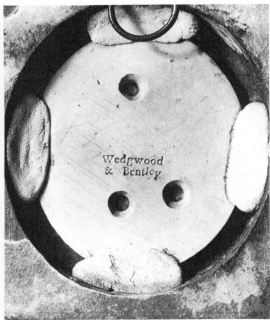

Portrait of Sully in contemporary frame. Medallions like this, made between 1775 and 1785, were the best Wedgwood ever made. Light blue jasper body with darker blue wash. White relief. Front of medallion shows intricate relief. Reverse, mark and firing holes. Height, 3in. Width, 2¾in. [Klamkin]

52

Blue jasper medallion.
White relief. Subject:
T h r e e   G r a c e s.
Marked: Wedgwood.
Nineteenth   century.
Diameter, 2in. [Klam-
kin]

by the ancient Greeks and Romans. After numerous trial pieces, he was able to produce a stoneware, opaque and hard, from which he could make bas reliefs in white, with various coloured backgrounds obtained by adding colouring oxides to the white clay mixture. Firing brought out the colours in the clay body. The bas relief was made by pressing the clay into intaglio moulds and applying the models by hand to the coloured clay body. There are to be seen at Barlaston 10,000 jasper trials made by Wedgwood while he experimented in jasperware, and it is thought that many more were destroyed.

The method for making bas relief jasperware has not changed much since the eighteenth century. The basic difference between early and modern pieces of jasper is in the hardness of the fired clay itself. The amount of finishing and undercutting (hand-trimming), a painstaking process that must be done by someone with the talent of a sculptor, would make jasperware of eighteenth-century quality prohibitively expensive for today's market. Presentation pieces of fine quality are made from time to time, but compared to Wedgwood and Bentley's jasper, modern jasperware leaves much to be desired.

There were two types of coloured jasperware made in the eighteenth century: the first is a solid jasper body that has colouring oxides throughout; and the second is a white jasper body that has been dipped or brushed with a slip of coloured clay. The jasper dip or 'wash' was considered by Wedgwood to have been the more successful of the two. He wrote to Bentley to say that he considered the jasper wash 'by far the finest grounds we ever made'. Wedgwood experimented with the colouring

53

(above) *Jasper dip taper holder in shape of Roman oil lamp. Blue with white relief. Marked: Wedgwood. C1780. Diameter, 3¼in. [Spero Collection]*; (left) *Perfume bottle of dark blue jasper with white relief. Silver top. Unmarked. C1785. Height, 3in. [Kaplan]*

of the fields for his bas reliefs. Many shades of blue can be seen in the small jasperware items of the early period, the differences in colour often depending on conditions in firing, the atmosphere, and the amount of cobalt added to the white clay body. Wedgwood also wrote of 'a beautiful Sea Green, and several other colours' as early as 1774.

At first the jasper body was used only for small gems, but experimentation in firing larger slabs of jasper continued at the same time. The firing of large slabs of clay is often difficult. The shrinkage of clay in firing depends on many factors, and the larger bas reliefs presented a problem in that there were two or more slightly different clay formulae being fired at the same time on the same piece. The research involved in perfecting large tablets and vases is staggering. The fact that all manner of items in jasperware were soon being produced and marketed throughout the western world is an indication of the determination and genius of Josiah Wedgwood.

His innate talent in the use of colour deserves mention, for it is often the judicious use of colour and shadings that gives his jasperware the uniqueness that is obvious when it is displayed next to the work of some of his imitators. Blue, in a very light shade, marks the earliest attempts at colouring and the Wedgwood and Bentley period is typified by a slightly richer hue. Vases made later, after Bentley's death in 1780, are of a somewhat darker shade of blue. The shades often varied because of conditions in firing, but they are always a true colour and were never faded or washed out in appearance.

The use of a combination of cobalt and iron led to green; several shades of sea-green, sage green and, the rarest, olive green, are also found in early period jasper. Other colours used were lilac, yellow and black. It is thought that the pink, peach and brownish hues that have been found were accidents occurring in trying for lilac. The unusual colours and shadings in old jasperware make it the highest priced of any of this ware.

Wedgwood realised the need for good modellers and sculptors for his jasper and hired William Hackwood, while Bentley employed John Flaxman. These two men

Green jasper dip 'Acanthus and Bell' bowl with white applied decoration. Marked: Wedgwood. C1790. Diameter, 10in. [Klamkin]

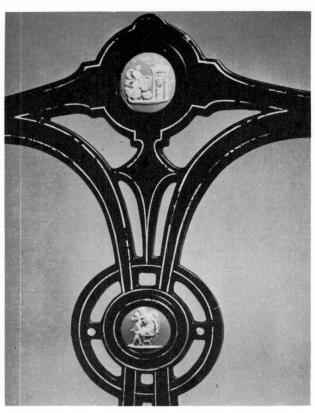

Papier-mâché chair set with two Wedgwood cameos. Label on chair sets time of manufacture between 1864 and 1870. Chair is black lacquer with hand-painted lines in white. Style is Victorian revival of Classic period. Close-up view shows cameos, which are blue with white relief. Height of top medallion, 2in. Diameter of lower medallion, 1½in. [Klamkin]

worked with other artists and modellers of note including James Tassie, George Stubbs, and Lady Templeton who designed some of the bas reliefs.

In most of the early portrait medallions of the Wedgwood and Bentley period, the wash method of colouring was used with great success. A blue wash was spread on a lighter blue body. The bas relief of this period has a wax-like density and 'feel'. One has only to handle a Wedgwood and Bentley portrait medallion of this nature to know that it is the zenith of the potter's art.

Along with the large jasperware plaques of the eighteenth century, perhaps the most desirable and sought after jasper is that made in combinations of more than two colours. Many of the small medallions and cameos were made in two, rarely three, colours in relief on a base of a contrasting colour. This type of jasper is usually of the highest quality. Three-colour jasper, which is seen more often, usually dates to a later period—1915–35. During this period white jasper with lilac and green relief was made, and this ware is almost as desirable and collectable as some

56

of the eighteenth-century ware. Eighteenth-century Wedgwood three-colour jasperware is so rare it is seldom seen anywhere but in museums.

Jasperware made in the years since the death of its inventor has varied enormously in quality, but has never been as successful artistically as it was in the eighteenth and early nineteenth centuries. After that the most collectable jasper has had unusual colours or colour combinations. Perhaps the most desirable is the crimson made between 1925 and 1932. Artistically, the crimson colour was unsuccessful, for the red colouring of many of the pieces bled during the firing, turning the white bas relief into pink.

(right) *White jasper three-handled mug. Green relief. Marked: Wedgwood, England. Height, 5in. [Klamkin]; (below) Dark blue jasper-dip tea-set. Marked: Wedgwood, England. C1930. Height of teapot, 5in. [Klamkin]*

Between 1920 and 1930 a dark olive green gave the Etruria potters a similar problem of bleeding. Only a little was made, and it is much desired by collectors today. The green bled so badly in most of these items that the 'white' bas relief is often green itself, creating extremely unattractive pieces. This type of jasper has the same kind of appeal for collectors that misprinted stamps or imperfectly minted coins do for philatelists or numismatists.

Jasperware has been made in other colours at various times: yellow, made from Wedgwood's day until 1850; buff, a lighter shade than the yellow, made from 1900 until 1930; and black (not to be confused with basalt), used in combination with yellow at the beginning of this century. A very rare colour, turquoise, was used in 1875 and wares in it are extremely rare today.

Once the jasper body was perfected, Wedgwood used it for many different items. Cameo medallions were highly successful. Likenesses of notables, living and dead, were made in many sizes and colours, although the combination of blue and white was the most common. Since there was no photography in the eighteenth century, these Wedgwood jasper cameos are often the only portraits we have of Wedgwood's contemporaries. His modellers took great pains with these likenesses and, while

(left) Blue jasper-dip biscuit jar with silver lid and handle. Yellow and white relief. Marked: Wedgwood. Although biscuit jars are common, the use of three colours makes this one unusual. Height, 5½in. [Klamkin]; (right) Light blue jasper-dip clock with white relief. Marked: Wedgwood, England. Height 8½in. [Jo-Anne Blum, Inc]

Buff jasperware pitcher with enamelled decoration and black lines. Marked: Wedgwood. Early twentieth century. Height, 3¼in. [Klamkin]

many were romanticised, for the most part each of these early portraits is a work of art and an important historical record.

Small medallions, seals in intaglio and cameos were the earliest objects made in jasperware, followed by tablets, busts, bell pulls, jewellery, vases, pots of all kinds, plates, cups and saucers (made for display, not for use), flower and bulb pots, teasets, paint boxes with fittings, toilet sets . . . in short, just about any small item. Larger objects that could not be made of jasperware were inset with medallions. Desks, work boxes, scales, clocks, cabinets, chairs and lamps were decorated with jasperware, which became popular the world over.

THE PORTLAND VASE

The original ancient glass vase belonged to the Barbarini family in Italy in the seventeenth century; and Sir William Hamilton bought it when he was ambassador in Naples and later sold it to the Duchess of Portland. Her son bought it from her estate at auction and lent it to Josiah Wedgwood for copying. The vase was not originally thought to have been glass, but onyx or some other hard stone. It is black-blue and opaque, overlaid with white glass which has been carved.

Wedgwood assigned his artists William Hackwood and William Wood to the job. The method of approach was, of necessity, exactly the opposite from the way the original vase must have been made. Moulds were made of the sculpted motifs so that these could be applied in the manner of all bas relief jasperware. Colouring and tex-

Copy of Portland vase made by Wedgwood. This vase has been made in many sizes and shapes throughout Wedgwood's history. Height, 10¼in. [Jo-Anne Blum, Inc]

ture also presented problems, because it was necessary to develop a clay body that would have the opaqueness and hardness of the glass, in the right colour. A 'Barbarini black' with traces of blue was developed and experimented with until something closely resembling the original colour was found.

The reproduction of the Portland Vase took Wedgwood close to four years and the first vases were ready by 1790. It is not known exactly how many copies were produced in the first place, but it was no more than forty-five. The British Museum, the Victoria and Albert Museum, the Wedgwood Museum at Barlaston, the Lady Lever Art Gallery and the Fogg Museum in Boston, Mass, all have copies.

Many re-issues of the first Portland vase have been made by Wedgwood since, but few of them were serious attempts at perfection. These vases have been made in every popular jasper colour or combination of colours. Wedgwood's reproduction of the Portland Vase was the high point in his career. What he lost in money was undoubtedly made up in the satisfaction at having accomplished what was thought to be impossible.

BONE CHINA

Josiah Wedgwood died in 1795 at the age of 64. He had never been able to produce bone china, for patents held by Champion had prevented him. When the factory, under Josiah II, did produce it in 1812 it was not a commercial success, and production continued for only ten years or so.

Bone china, or porcelain, is a mixture of clay and bone ash which is highly fired and requires no glaze. A variety of porcelain had been made in China and imported to England in the eighteenth century where it became popular among those who could afford it. Although he was unable to produce the china without infringing Champion's patent for the use of Cornish clay, Josiah I was able to capture some of the market for white china by his manufacture of pearlware.

Although Josiah II was artistically successful in the manufacture of bone china, he could not compete with the French. Dessert and tea services had been made and

Bone - china inkwells, sander and stand. Hand-decorated. Marked: Wedgwood (outline of Portland Vase). C1900. Length, 8in. Width, 4in. Height, 2in. [Jo-Anne Blum, Inc]

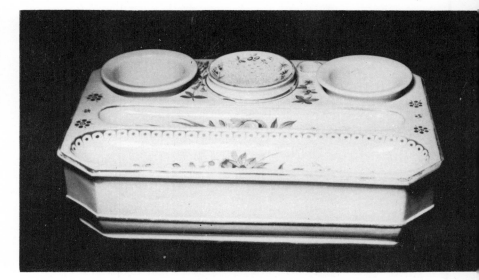

Bone-china box with silver-plated base and lid. Ivory finial. China insert is printed and hand-painted. Marked: Wedgwood (outline of Portland Vase). C1880. Length of insert, 5¼in. Width, 4¼in. Height, 2in. [Klamkin]

Bone-china tea-set, hand-painted decoration. Green with silver lustre borders on white. Probably designed by Victor Skellern around 1940. Height of pot, 9in. [Jo-Anne Blum, Inc]

Bone-china cake plate, banded with silver. The design, by Eric Ravilious, is 'Persephone'. This pattern was designed with the Queen's seal in the centre for the coronation banquet service. Marked: Wedgwood, Bone China, Made in England (Portland Vase outline). 1953. Diameter, 12in. [Klamkin]

when the company discontinued production, Spode was commissioned to make re-placements for customers. Early Wedgwood bone china is, therefore, very rarely found and even the museums do not have much. The mark on early bone china is imprinted in small letters in red, gold or blue overglaze, sometimes with an accompanying impressed mark.

The second period of Wedgwood bone china production began in 1878, in the high Victorian period, and in styles to match. It is worth collecting. This second period of bone china production is marked with a replica of the Portland Vase and this mark, or a variation of it, is still used to mark Wedgwood bone china today.

Many items made at the end of the nineteenth century could not have been made during any other period, and these are worth watching for. A bone-china box insert in a Sheffield silver stand with a silver cover, for instance, could only be Victorian, and is a collectable item. There are many decorative bone-china patterns that were discontinued because they became outmoded, and it is these very patterns that are most representative of their time, and interesting to the china collector.

Modern bone china made by Wedgwood contains about 45 per cent of bone ash and is a strong white translucent body. It is made in both traditional and modern shapes, some plates being made with rims and others in the coup shape (though this is beginning to look dated). In 1936 a porcelain body was made to which a pink

Bone-china tea-set in award-winning 'Asia' lithograph pattern. This pattern, a modified Greek key design, was originally made in three colours, but the black and gold has proved to be the most popular. 1956. Height of pot, 9in. [Klamkin]

(left) Light blue lustre vase with Chinese-inspired decoration. Height, 6in. [Jo-Anne Blum, Inc]; (right) Pair of 'Dragon Lustre' vases. Blue mottled glaze with gold-printed dragons. Height, 8in. [Klamkin]

colouring was added, and this ware is called 'Alpine Pink'. Before World War I a group of artists assembled at the factory to reproduce, free-hand, designs from the first Josiah's pattern book and to originate new designs and patterns. The resulting hand-painted items in bone china are sought after by collectors. The established method of decorating china at the Wedgwood factory today includes the use of transfer patterns, multicolour lithography and on-glaze enamel painting. Many patterns still require freehand decoration in the finishing.

In 1908 the Wedgwood firm succeeded in producing on their bone china the old Chinese 'powder blue' as a decorative glaze, and lustred china was made about this time also. Both these types have become collector's items.

Since there has always been more earthenware produced than china and bone china has not until the past eighty years or so been produced to any large extent, there is a shortage of even the later production for the collector. Even today less than a third of the company's production is china, the rest being earthenware and stoneware, though china, being more expensive when new, brings in the same amount of money.

The one type of bone china that has recently become extremely desirable, despite the fact that it is not even of antique value, is the lustreware made at the beginning of this century. Decorative items of particular beauty and artistic importance have

64

rocketed in price, though such vases, bowls, etc, were not inexpensive to begin with. Between the introduction of the 'powder blue' glaze and 1932, other magnificent one-of-a-kind lustres were turned out, in part under the influence of the art nouveau movement in England and partly through a renewed interest in ceramic glazes.

The person responsible for the most magnificent of these lustre pieces was Daisy Makeig-Jones, who designed lustrewares in fanciful 'Fairyland' style. She also used designs derived in part from Chinese and Japanese art, though many had Persian overtones as well. This strange combination of influences led to many unique and handsome bone-china decorations. The bone china, itself, is highly fired and trans-lucent, and looks particularly fine when held up to a strong light.

Miss Makeig-Jones's style is probably most easily categorised as 'Art Deco', that movement which followed closely on art nouveau. The Wedgwood firm turned out numerous art objects that were individual and different, but similar in style. There were many pairs of vases, but no two are really identical, the lustre glaze being individual on each piece.

Dragon lustre, fairyland lustre or any of the other lustres of this period are all very beautiful. Unfortunately, there was too little made to satisfy the present demand, for this ware is sought by collectors of fine china everywhere. The decorations include birds, butterflies, dragons, dancing fairies and fairyland scenes, and the ware is marked with the backstamp of the Portland vase in gold.

Wedgwood bone china of any period is worth collecting. Search for patterns that are representative of the decorative periods since 1878. These plates, dishes and vases promise to be the antiques of the future.

Pair of vases in bone china. Fairyland lustre with interesting motifs. Persian - inspired borders in gold. Height, 9in. [Spero Collection]

6
Commemorative Ware

In the days of Josiah Wedgwood, when there was no photography, landscape scenes were often copied from surrounding areas and either painted directly or transfer-printed on plates. Often these form pictorial records of parts of eighteenth-century England and complement paintings and drawings. Many porcelain and pottery companies since Wedgwood's time have produced landscape patterns, some imagined and many real. Wedgwood, however, developed in 1880 a unique branch of pottery decoration and distribution that still continues. Plates and dishes commemorating

Bone-china tea-set, 'Liberty China' pattern. This was the only commemorative china made by Wedgwood during World War I. Height of teapot to finial, 5in. [Mattatuck Museum]

(above) *Creamware commemorative tray with blue applied relief, and reverse of tray showing mark and legend. Diameter, 6in. [Jo-Anne Blum, Inc]; (right) Creamware plate. One of series of four; design engraved in black from illustration by artist, Clare Leighton. While Miss Leighton's 'New England Series' is well-known to collectors of commemoratives, these plates from Bennett College are not. Diameter, 10in. [Leighton]*

special anniversaries, places or events are produced in limited quantities for the American market. These plates are made to order, usually in Queen's ware, and record events of historical importance, anniversaries of buildings, cities, colleges, universities and other organisations. About 100 new designs of this type are introduced every year. Usually, the design is a photo-engraving of one or more buildings of an institution and the plates are sold at college bookstores or elsewhere to raise money for a particular cause. Many of the special commemorative issues of bone china and earthenware, though not very old, have become collector's items also.

(top left) *Creamware plate, showing Stratford Hall in Virginia, birthplace of Robert E. Lee. Printed in mulberry colour. Diameter, 9in.* [*Klamkin*]; (top right) *Printed creamware commemorative plate showing Empire State Building in New York. Diameter, 10in.* [*Schaffer Collection*]; (above) *Creamware commemorative plate for Canada. One of a series. Also legend on reverse. Diameter, 10in.* [*Klamkin*]

Perhaps the first important 'special issue' was the great Queen's ware service that Wedgwood made for the Empress Catherine of Russia. This dinner service, consisting of 952 pieces, was commissioned by the Empress in 1774 and each piece was hand–painted with a different view of famous houses, castles, abbeys and outdoor scenes in England. The views were painted by many different artists and the plates were adorned with an oak border and the Royal Frog Crest. The design and decoration exercised Wedgwood's talents to the utmost, but the resulting publicity was well worth the effort. The 'Empress Catherine' shape, designed specially for this set of dishes, was used afterwards for Queen's ware designs and patterns. The set was put on display in Wedgwood's London showroom before it was shipped to Russia.

The Wedgwood company's connections with royalty have always been important and commemorative ware of coronations and other special royal events are keenly sought. For the coronation of Queen Elizabeth II, the firm issued special jasperware in a shade of blue that had never been used before, and the tea-set commemorating the coronation is already a collector's item. Coronation pottery and china cannot be made for a period longer than six months following the event and, therefore, all coronation souvenirs are limited in the amounts issued.

One particularly interesting 'special issue', which is now part of the history of American and British relations, is Wedgwood's china and Queen's ware in the Liberty pattern. In 1917 an American anglophile, Mrs Robert Coleman Taylor, of New York, decided to raise money for a group of British charities. She decided that

Creamware monteith designed for the Wedgwood Club of Boston in honour of twentieth anniversary of club. This type of commemorative ware, made in limited editions, is desired by American collectors. Length, 12in. [Schaffer Collection]

Teapot. Royal blue jasper made for Queen Elizabeth II Coronation in 1953. This shade of blue was used only this one time. Height, 5½in. [Coe Collection]

perhaps a 'special issue' of Wedgwood china to be sold by subscription only should be commissioned and Josiah Wedgwood & Sons agreed to supply it. Mrs Taylor and her friends designed a pattern consisting of the American shield in the midst of the Allied flags, with the flags of England and France at the top, the flag of Belgium between them, and a wreath of laurel to surround the shield. The only other decoration was a narrow band of gold on the edges of the dishes.

The first set of 'Liberty China' arrived in September 1917, and orders were taken by Mrs Taylor in her home. In all, 4,983 pieces of china were delivered and sold and 4,266 pieces of Queen's ware. Mrs Taylor raised $14,203.14 for her war charities.

During World War II Josiah Wedgwood & Sons produced commemorative plates called 'Old London Scenes' on their own initiative in order to raise money for the British War Relief. There were twelve plates in the series, hand-engraved in sepia on the 'Edme' shape. Some of the scenes portrayed were the Tower of London and Tower Bridge, Westminster Abbey, the Guildhall, the Houses of Parliament, and St James's Palace. The series was sold in America for $24.00, with $4.00 of this price being donated to British War Relief.

In 1930 a set of commemorative plates called The American College Series was issued. This was a result of a co-operative effort between Josiah Wedgwood & Sons and Jones, McDuffee & Stratton, their American representatives, together with the American artists who designed the series. Specially marked first editions of these plates are highly collectable today. Colleges represented in this series are Harvard, Bowdoin, Mount Holyoke, University of Michigan, St Paul's School, Princeton, Wellesley, Smith, West Point, Vassar, University of Pennsylvania, Wesleyan, Yale, Denison, MIT, Columbia and the University of California.

Highly prized today by collectors is a series of New England historical scenes that were issued about 1905. Included in this series are Faneuil Hall, the Old State House, Old North Church, the Boston 'Tea Party', the Return of the Mayflower and John Alden and Priscilla.

Perhaps the most outstanding series for the American market was that designed in 1952 by Clare Leighton, a British artist who has made New England her home. Miss Leighton was commissioned by Wedgwood to design twelve wood-cuts from which engravings could be made to commemorate New England industries. These plates, produced in a limited number, have already become collector's items.

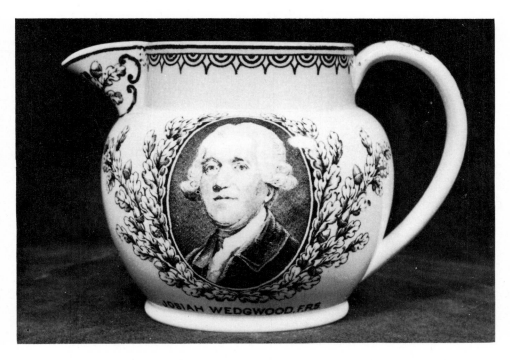

Wedgwood commemorative pitcher, creamware, printed in black. Portraying Josiah Wedgwood. Height, 4in. [Klamkin]

7
Wedgwood Production after 1850

By the middle of the nineteenth century, Wedgwood's customers had obviously had too much of a good thing and interest in neo-classic design waned. Josiah Wedgwood, the man, was remembered by several devotees who wrote his biography. However, the quality of jasperware and jasper-dipped ware declined alarmingly: there are many examples of blistered and peeled jasper dip vases made from the original moulds that could never be mistaken for the careful earlier work.

In 1885, however, white jasper vases with bas relief in lilac and green were introduced, and these were respectable in every way. Jasperware portrait medallions also were made throughout the nineteenth century, though not in the great quantities of the earlier period, for the development of photography had reduced the market.

The neo-classic period was well over by the mid-nineteenth century and the styles that were so highly developed by Josiah Wedgwood and then his son became outmoded, except for a brief revival in the late Victorian period. Victorian-influenced neo–classicism differed somewhat from the earlier period, being more an adaptation

Rockingham glaze teapot. This brown glaze is difficult to find in marked Wedgwood. Widow finial on cover. Late nineteenth century. Marked: Wedgwood. Height, 5in. [Klamkin]

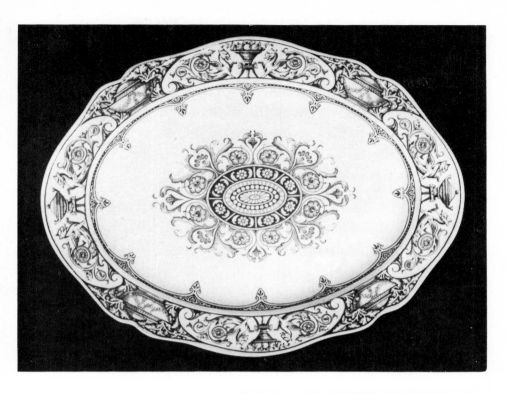

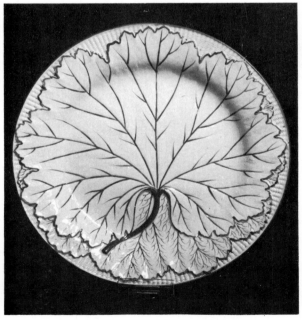

(above) *Pearlware platter.*
Blue printed under-glaze
design. Marked: Wedg-
wood. 1893. Length, 19in.
[Klamkin]; (right) Cream-
ware plate. Embossed leaf
pattern outlined by hand in
green. Marked: Wedgwood.
Early nineteenth century.
[Jo-Anne Blum, Inc]

Four tiles. Printed in brown. Characters from A Midsummer
Night's Dream. *Marked: Wedgwood & Sons, Etruria. C1870–1902.
Size, 6in square.* [Jo-Anne Blum, Inc]

and less a direct copy. The Victorians put their own stamp on the jasperware and
basalt made during this period. In 1875 the Wedgwood company made vases of
basalt decorated with gold slipware applied in leaf and vine patterns, which cannot
be mistaken for anything but Victorian.

Collectable jasperware and basalt of the latter half of the nineteenth century,
therefore, is original work designed for the contemporary market. Much of its workmanship leaves something to be desired, but it is of importance historically and
artistically, nevertheless. Some of it is beautiful, though the harsh blue used for
much of the jasper dip does not appeal to many collectors and often the vases are
overdecorated for modern tastes.

About 1870, the Wedgwood firm opened a tile department in order to enter a
steady and what they hoped would prove a profitable market. The tiles of this
period, largely decorated with transfer-printed designs, have become highly collectable. Many recently found are amusingly decorated with scenes from fairy tales or
with Kate Greenaway children, and embossed on the reverse, 'Josiah Wedgwood &
Sons, Etruria'. The Wedgwood tile business was not a commercial success, however, and was abandoned in 1902.

In 1870 Victoria ware was introduced. This new body was identified by Harry Buten as 'half way between bone china and Queen's ware'. At the same time a buff-coloured bone china decorated with gold slip and painted in the style of Worcester china appeared, as did a peach-coloured stoneware.

Parian ware, a totally different clay body from any Wedgwood had made before, was introduced in 1848. This unglazed porcelain, which looked like marble, was used to make statuary, particularly of Victorian notables. The modellers used were Victorian sculptors and most of Wedgwood's Parian pieces were signed by the artist as well as bearing the impressed mark of the firm. Many of the moulds used for basalt busts in the eighteenth century were quite adaptable to the Parian ware.

Between 1858 and 1875, Emile Lessore, a French artist, was given complete freedom to experiment with ceramic colours, which he painted free-hand directly on specially designed Queen's ware pieces. He alone was responsible for continuing the practice of artist-decorated ceramics at Wedgwood in an era when the machine and mass production had completely taken over this field. He is considered the

(left) *Blue jasper plaque of George Washington. Likeness was taken from medal designed in France by Voltaire. It was common to depict dignitaries as Roman emperors in late eighteenth century. Wedgwood issued other likenesses in bas relief of Washington but this was the first, dating to 1777. Marked: Washington, Wedgwood, O. [Klamkin]; (right) Portrait medallion of Bergman (a friend of Darwin's) modelled by Flaxman. Body of medallion is pale blue jasper but front surface and portrait are waxy white. Marked: Wedgwood and Bentley. Height, 5in. Width, 3½in. [Kaplan]*

Enamelled bough pot, gold lustre decoration. Marked: Wedgwood (outline of Portland Vase). Early twentieth century. Height, 8in. [Jo-Anne Blum, Inc]

oustanding ceramic decorator of the nineteenth century. However, since he was an artist and could decorate relatively little of the total Wedgwood production, other methods of decorating were tried. Lithography was first used in 1863 and while it was hardly a substitute for free-hand decoration, it has been constantly improved so that it is now a tasteful and artistically successful method of plate decoration.

The reintroduction of bone china in 1878 was an attempt by the management at Wedgwood to resuscitate the efforts of Josiah Wedgwood II. This time the new product met with success and currently is an important segment of the firm's business.

In all, there was much experimentation in pottery and china production during the latter half of the nineteenth century and while some of the clay bodies, shapes and designs made have continued profitably for Wedgwood's, other more quickly abandoned lines make up a list of scarce and collectable items for today's Wedgwood enthusiast. Some may be still waiting to be discovered. There was a certain frenzy about the Wedgwood company's experimentation at this period, for it was not as sound financially as it had been.

76

8
Majolica

Majolica, a product in which the technique is to use an opaque shiny glaze to achieve rich brilliant colours and the appearance of a heavy body, was made by Wedgwood between 1860 and 1910. All Victorian majolica is now being avidly collected. Majolica is one category of Wedgwood collecting in which the collector will be able to gather an interesting and increasingly valuable collection quite cheaply. As with most pottery of the past 200 years, if it is marked 'Wedgwood' it will be more valuable than a comparable unmarked piece.

Majolica game-pie dish. Crossed rifles form finial. Brown, green and yellow glaze. Marked: Wedgwood. Late nineteenth century. Length, 10in. [Jo-Anne Blum, Inc]

(left) *Majolica ale jug. Tan background with brown and blue flower motifs incised. Late nineteenth century. Height, 10in. [Jo-Anne Blum, Inc]; (right) Majolica plant or flower holder. 'Somnus' is typical of adornment adapted from eighteenth-century jasper and basalt. Marked: Wedgwood. Late nineteenth century. Height, 9in. [Jo-Anne Blum, Inc]*

Collectors of early vintage Wedgwood disdain its late nineteenth-century majolica, yet there is much to be said in its favour as a collectable item. While a good deal of the nineteenth-century majolica was made of dark clay, the Wedgwood factory used its Queen's ware body, and so the relief is much more precise and finer than the rest. The soft lead glaze is stained with colouring oxides to produce brilliant colour effects, which make the plates, compotes, plaques, etc, highly decorative. And because of the method used to mark nineteenth-century wares by Wedgwood, this ware is easily dated.

Unlike much Victorian majolica, Wedgwood was not copied from Italian Renaissance pottery, but often appeared in refreshing new shapes, both amusing and attractive. New items of Wedgwood majolica are constantly turning up, because little research has been done on it by writers on Wedgwood. Most common are the green-glazed plates with leaf designs in relief, a type made consistently throughout the history of the factory and, therefore, not strictly speaking Victoriana. The originals were the green-glazed ware of the Wedgwood-Whieldon period.

Many of the shapes and decorations in majolica are elaborate adaptations of earlier Wedgwood motifs. In some pieces the work and decorations are a little crude, the more so when the piece was made to be useful rather than decorative. It was not orginally an expensive ware, though there are many elaborate display pieces that must have been a large enough investment originally. All Wedgwood majolica has beautiful glazes, the colours are true and rich, and the shapes are often very graceful.

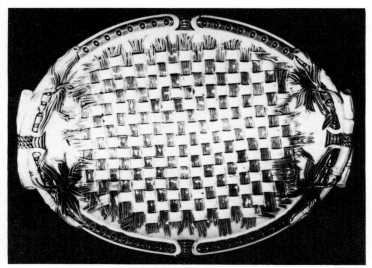

(above) *Majolica tray. Embossed and painted decoration to give effect of basket weaving. Marked: Wedgwood. Late nineteenth century. Length, 14in. [Jo-Anne Blum, Inc]*; (below) *Highest quality majolica that Wedgwood made. Left, tankard with cobalt glaze. Right, plate with pierced edge in Chinese motif. Embossed birds, flowers and butterflies with brilliant glazes. Both marked: Wedgwood. Late nineteenth century. Diameter of plate, 10in. Height of tankard, 8in. [Jo-Anne Blum, Inc]*

(above left) *Majolica plate. Cream colour background with pink, blue and green decoration. Marked: Wedgwood. 1882. Diameter, 7½in. [Klamkin];* (above right) *Majolica wall plaque. Cream-colour figure with blue background. Self-framed. Relief work is high and well done. Marked: Wedgwood. Late nineteenth century. Diameter, 10in. [Jo-Anne Blum, Inc];* (left) *Green majolica plate using* email ombrant *technique as decoration. Judicious use of relief and enamel creates effect of deep relief. Marked: Wedgwood. C1860–1900. Diameter, 8¾in. [Jo-Anne Blum, Inc]*

Items made in Wedgwood majolica ware include game-pie dishes (some of which were made in the same moulds used for caneware), umbrella stands, wall brackets, pitchers, compotes, planters, spittoons, wall plaques and plates and dishes of various shapes and sizes.

Although a large amount of Wedgwood majolica was produced, the demand for it has recently increased, so the value is apt to rise rather rapidly. This ware was produced in many shapes and designs by many potters, and it is not always easily recognisable as Wedgwood. Sometimes the mark is obscured by the depth of the glaze, and needs close inspection. If the word 'Wedgwood' can be found on a piece of Victorian majolica, buy it. It is a collector's item of the future and well worth displaying today.

9
Collectable Twentieth-century Wedgwood

The art styles of the turn of the century were again reflected in Wedgwood pottery. In the second half of the nineteenth century William Morris had advocated a return to hand-crafting and the manufacture of artist-designed accessories for the home. A new style in home decoration called Art Nouveau emerged.

The philosophy of this new movement—to incorporate the talents of the artist and artisan in producing new wares in an entirely different art style from any that had gone before—was artistically exciting. In this tradition, Wedgwood hired Alfred and Louise Powell and Thérèse Lessore to decorate by hand art pottery and also to

Shell-shaped compote painted and signed by Emile Lessore. Marked: Wedgwood. Diameter, 8in. C1872. [Spero Collection]

81

Basalt boar designed for Wedgwood by John Skeaping in 1927. Skeaping did a series of small animals in basalt which are now sought by collectors. Height, 4½in. [Schaffer Collection]

teach the decorators hand-techniques in painting. Both Louise Powell and her sister, Thérèse, were grand-daughters of Emile Lessore. They established the school and also decorated some pieces individually, but these pieces, by necessity, were few.

At the beginning of this century also a revival of eighteenth-century shapes and forms of decoration took place, particularly in America, and the Wedgwood firm experimented with and produced a few pieces in unusual colours and combinations of colour in their jasperware. We are still too close to the art of this period to evaluate it, and the Wedgwood pottery and china made in this century is not yet old enough to have antique value, so it has not been collected in any quantity. However, the crimson jasperware as well as the dark olive green mentioned previously are almost as expensive currently as fine eighteenth-century jasperware. While experimentation in new patterns and styles continued, Wedgwood also made traditional patterns and designed new borders for many of their traditional shapes. As had been done in the past, the patterns incorporated the use of transfer printing and free-hand painting, but the painting was now done on an assembly-line and required little creative talent from the artists. No large pottery firm could now afford to turn out hand-crafted products in large amounts, even if enough talented artists were available; so Wedgwood turned to the designer-artist, to engraving and lithography for tableware decoration.

The art director from 1902 to 1934 was J. E. Goodwin. It was under his direction that the magnificent lustreware designed by Miss Makeig-Jones was created. Many of the bone china shapes for this ware were original, but eighteenth-century creamware shapes were also used.

Fairyland lustre plate. Designed and decorated by Daisy Makeig-Jones between 1915 and 1932. Marked: Wedgwood (Portland Vase outline in gold). Made in England. Diameter, 10in. [Spero Collection]

Bone-china bowl. Lustre with circus motifs. Bright yellow interior with black animal designs. Gold designs on black, yellow and cream lustre on outside of bowl. This is an unusual and particularly effective example of Miss Makeig-Jones' style of decoration. Diameter, 8½in. [Coe Collection]

Goodwin was succeeded by Victor Skellern. Keith Murray, an architect, was hired in 1933 to create new forms that would be adaptable to contemporary mass production, and body and shape become once again more important than decoration. Two-colour slipware was made in new as well as in traditional shapes. An Alpine pink colour for fine china was introduced in 1939 and the dark blue jasperware of the nineteenth century was discontinued. New matte glazes in several colours were also introduced, and at first were left undecorated. 'Form follows function' became the motto of the modernists and Keith Murray's undecorated well shaped pottery is typical of this period.

Creamware plate. Blue printed decoration, showing Yale University, USA. Although made in 1949, this plate has already become a collector's item. Length, 12in. Width, 9½in. [Klamkin]

Bone-china ear-rings. The Wedgwood Company made bone-china jewellery in 1963 for a short period. This jewellery is already sought after by Wedgwood collectors. Diameter, ⅞in. [Jo-Anne Blum, Inc]

84

10
Wedgwood Imitators and Imitations

While imitation may be the most sincere form of flattery, a man who makes his living by the production of a unique product is inclined to call it plagiarism. Josiah Wedgwood and his successors in the company suffered more than most. Wedgwood ware has been imitated for 200 years, sometimes well, sometimes badly. The collector, therefore, has to be careful.

The best known imitations of Wedgwood are the jasperware products made at the time of Josiah Wedgwood's first commercial success with his own. Some of these pieces by Adams, Neale, Turner and others are quite good and worth owning as long as the collector knows what he is buying. The best of these are signed by their makers and their value is often as high as comparable Wedgwood, except to the Wedgwood collector.

In 1769 the two potters, Neale and Turner, copied one of Wedgwood's encaustic vases and when accused of this asserted that the painted design was taken from a print by Hamilton and, therefore, they had as much right to it as Wedgwood. An out-of-court settlement would indicate that they were probably right and the two potters afterwards shared the patent for the design with Wedgwood. He continued to make encaustic painted wares and his talent generally outshone that of other contemporary potters.

Potters in France and Germany copied Wedgwood's medallions with varying degrees of success. When these medallions were applied to furniture and other items, there was often no certain method of recognising their makers. But probably most of the applied medallions were made by Wedgwood, as he produced so many.

In the 1930s a flood of imitation Wedgwood was imported into America from Germany and Japan. It was generally very badly made, but was sold in antique as well as gift shops. It did not have the Wedgwood mark, but the 'Made in Germany' or 'Made in Japan' marks were sometimes scraped out or stamped over with the name of the importer or dealer and the ware was sold as 'Old Wedgwood'. This practice was difficult to control, but the Wedgwood company was able to obtain an injunction to keep these imitations from being advertised as Wedgwood, which the importers maintained was a generic name. The German and Japanese imitations of Wedgwood jasperware are usually moulded in one piece to give the effect of bas relief, which, on true Wedgwood, is applied separately by hand to a turned body. The imitations, therefore, have indentations inside where the relief has been moulded, and are recognisable for what they are.

More difficult to detect are those ceramics made during the early nineteenth century and marked 'Wedgewood' by William Smith & Co. The same company also used the mark 'Queen's Ware'. Josiah Wedgwood & Sons were granted a court injunction to stop this practice, which was obviously designed to cash in on Wedgwood's success. The false mark was not used after 1848.

The following marks are not the marks of Josiah Wedgwood's firm: 'J. Wedgwood', the mark of John Wedge Wood; 'Wedgwood & C.', the mark of the Unicorn & Pinnox Works, Tunstall, a company established in 1860 and still existing; the same mark used between 1796 and 1801 by the Ferrybridge Pottery in Yorkshire; and items marked 'Wedgwood & Co.' These marks can easily be detected by any careful collector.

There is another shady practice that is a problem for collectors and dealers alike. Collectors of early jasperware or basalt will not buy a piece if it is marked 'Made in England', a legend which dates from the passing of the McKinley Tariff Act of 1891. But many pieces of twentieth-century Wedgwood are being imported into the United States with this mark removed. Without the tell-tale mark, a dealer can claim that his Wedgwood is over 100 years old and, therefore, can be imported duty-free. The other reason behind this fraud is obvious, and it is not difficult to remove this impressed mark from most pieces of solid jasper or basalt. Of course, no specialist Wedgwood dealer would condone this practice. Fortunately, no one has, to my knowledge, found a satisfactory method for adding 'and Bentley' to the impressed Wedgwood mark, though as long ago as 1875, Eliza Meteyard warned that Wedgwood and Bentley bases were being used on new vases. But with all the above problems to consider when collecting old Wedgwood, there are still fewer worries than there are in collecting just about any other make or type of ceramics. Just remember to buy nothing that has not a bona-fide Wedgwood mark.

11
Condition and Repairs

One of the problems that will confront the collector from time to time is finding the rare piece he wanted, but not in perfect condition. A chip, often called 'flake' or 'check' by an auctioneer, will detract from the monetary value of any piece of pottery, but the avid collector is often faced with the choice of an imperfect piece or none at all. If the condition is not too bad or if the piece in question may be displayed in a cabinet with its fault to the back, it may be a worthwhile investment.

Wedgwood quality has often led past owners to repair broken pieces rather than discard them. In the days when expert repairing was more of an art than it is today and there were more capable repairers, many pieces of Wedgwood which we might not even today consider particularly valuable were repaired so well that only close examination will reveal the imperfection. People have, it seems, always become more attached to a piece of pottery if made by Wedgwood and have valued it enough to be willing to restore it. So the collector should inspect each piece of old Wedgwood he buys very carefully. Often a good repair will not be obvious until the piece has been owned and handled for a while. This is particularly true of Queen's ware. The true collector can only be grateful that a former owner thought enough of a piece to have gone to the trouble and expense of saving it.

If a repaired piece of old Wedgwood has been sold for perfect by any reputable dealer, he will always offer to return the purchase price if a repair is later brought to his attention. Usually a price adjustment can be made. Indeed, expert repairs are so expensive today that the dealer may point out that the piece should really be worth more.

One reason that the collector should be aware of all repairs is that this knowledge will have some bearing on how the pottery should be cleaned and handled. The strength of most Wedgwood pottery in pristine condition makes it possible for many of the creamware and china dishes to be put into automatic dishwashers, but obviously this shouldn't be done if there has been a repair.

Decorative Wedgwood, particularly jasperware with bas relief, requires regular washing; and it is best to use a mild soap and warm water solution. Where the relief has become discoloured or has collected dirt in the crevices, a soft toothbrush and ordinary soap will restore it to its original condition. Once again, inspect any newly acquired piece carefully for repairs. There is nothing more frightening than to see what appears to be part of the jasper dip peeling off before your eyes as you are washing an antique vase.

Pale blue jasper plaque with white relief. Designed by Lady Diana Beauclerc. Marked: Wedgwood. Diameter, 4in. [Kaplan]

If something is rare enough, the fact that it has been properly repaired will make little difference to its value. For instance, a large Wedgwood jasper vase or plaque, rare, beautiful and difficult to find, is worth owning whether or not it has been repaired. A good example of eighteenth-century jasperware is almost impossible to find in its original condition anyway, and a crack does not detract too much from its beauty. Plaques are often framed and protected from further damage and the handling will be minimal.

Any eighteenth-century Wedgwood should be restored and preserved. Like any work of art, one should feel an obligation to preserve the best examples. Many old plaques, urns, bowls and vases in some of the world's finest museums have obviously been broken and repaired.

Later Wedgwood is often worth proper restoration also. The useful wares are becoming scarce today because they were handled more often than the decorative pieces, so eighteenth-century Queen's ware should be cared for and preserved. There are still a few expert repair men left, though they are very expensive; but the increasing value of an important dish such as an early tureen or large platter makes it well worth saving. Another instance where an expensive repair might be in order is when one of a dozen favourite plates is broken and the probability of finding a matching one is slim.

Minor pieces in one's collection which are broken but do not warrant expert repair, can be saved by using one of the proprietary adhesives readily available. While any piece of ceramics repaired in this manner may not be washable, the glue will do for a cabinet piece and often will keep broken parts together until the pieces can be expertly repaired.

Over-glaze painting on early Queen's ware and pearlware must be cleaned very carefully. Such painting is simple enough to detect. Hold a piece of decorated pottery so that it catches the light from the side. If the decoration appears flat and seems to have been applied to the dish after it has been glazed, that is over-glaze painting. It has a tendency to chip and often a small chip will continue to flake off. Since some of the most charming old Wedgwood dishes have this kind of decoration, they should be used only as display pieces. They should be washed in warm (not hot) water by hand using mild suds, and dried carefully with a soft towel.

Since you have chosen Wedgwood collecting as a hobby, you will want to look at and handle your collection; and sooner or later you will break something. Never mind. Hunt for another piece like it. The joys of collecting Wedgwood must override the fact that it is breakable.

Cheese dish. Dark blue jasper dip, white bas relief. Marked: Wedgwood. Diameter of plate, 12in. Height, 10in. [Jo-Anne Blum, Inc]

12
Wedgwood and Flower Arranging

Josiah Wedgwood was a devotee of flowers, as we can see from his decorative use of flowers and foliage for his creamware. Berries, leaves and flowers of all kinds are used in his early border patterns on plates and vases. Besides using flowers as decoration, he was the first British potter to make flower pots for inside the house.

Flower pots of common red clay, much as we know them today, were being made in Wedgwood's day for outside use and, at first, Wedgwood concentrated on improving the design and quality of these. Grey and white stoneware pots were made

White jasper flower vase, chocolate brown bas relief. Marked: Wedgwood. C1810. Diameter, 6in. [Jo-Anne Blum, Inc]

Unusual three-colour smear-glaze white stoneware vase. Motifs are lilac and green on white ground. Marked: Wedgwood. Height, 4in. [Klamkin]

at this time also, and Wedgwood improved their appearance by adding enamelled colours and festoons and medallions in applied clay. As these pots became popular, Wedgwood saw the potentiality of the market, and produced almost every pattern he was then making in Queen's ware in his flower-pot and bough-pot shapes. Basalt and terra-cotta vases were then tried and proved successful. Pedestals, plinths, and stands of various shapes, sizes and types, were sold with his pots. By 1768 Wedgwood was doing an enormous business in flower pots. In his usual thorough fashion he had made a study of the types of flower holders and pots that floriculturists of his time might want and he experimented to perfect as many different practical and elegant vases as he could. There is evidence in Wedgwood's letters to Bentley that as the flower pots were made, Josiah's wife tried them out at home to see whether they were practical. The containers made included pots for growing bulbs and ferns as well as holders for cut flowers and branches.

As the fashion for bringing flowers inside the house grew, the variety of Wedgwood containers grew also. Caneware and Queen's ware tubular vases, already being made by some of Wedgwood's competitors, were produced and improved upon by Wedgwood. He made various kinds of bough pots in which to display bouquets of branches and flowers under (not on) tables and slabs, and pots in which to grow and display the various precious bulbs brought back by travellers from other countries. In the eighteenth century it was not customary for flowers to be placed on mantels as we do today and for mantel decoration Wedgwood made groups of jasper or basalt ornaments that did not need the enhancement of flowers. Indeed few jasperware vases are suitable for flowers, for the ware is ornamental enough in itself.

Pottery collecting and flower arranging are two complementary activities. Any flower devotee searches for the proper container to show off his prize roses. He also relieves his winter frustration by growing plants indoors, and the pots for these should be decorative without detracting from the beauty of the plant. Flower or plant containers for the home should also be able to hold water, and, in the case of growing plants, have the ability to absorb moisture. They should also be adaptable to many different kinds of plants and to different flower arrangements. Josiah

(left) *Creamware vase, engine-turned. Cover missing. Decorated in pale pink slip and brown hand-painting. Marked: Wedgwood (impressed). Eighteenth century. Height, 8½in. [Jo-Anne Blum, Inc]; (right) Creamware bough pot. Top pierced to hold stems or branches. Surface agate decoration and gilded. Marked: Wedgwood and Bentley. C1772. Height, 8in. [Schaffer Collection]*

Encaustic decorated basalt vase with free-hand decoration in red and white. Swan's heads at bases of handles. Marked: Wedgwood. C1775. Height, 10in. [Spero Collection]

Wedgwood understood these facts and the tradition of designing beautiful and practical flower containers is one that has continued throughout the company's history.

Wedgwood's 'Bulbous root pots' allowed flowering bulbs to be properly grown. They were designed so that the soil, water and bulb could be properly positioned, the bulb being held by bulb-shaped removable holders. These root pots were made in jasperware, basalt, caneware and drabware and are among the most beautiful of all early Wedgwood. Josiah I also made hedgehog crocus planters with underdishes; the bulbs were planted in soil inside the hedgehog and the spiky leaves grew out through the holes which cover the body of the animal.

Some eighteenth–century Wedgwood flower containers, made in a shape also used by other contemporary potters, consisted of fan-shaped groups of five small vases connected at the bottom. These containers showed off flowers to their best advantage and were very popular. Wedgwood also made vases shaped like tree trunks, and this natural asymmetrical line was later adopted by Art Nouveau artists. 'Ruin'd Columns' was another popular shape for vases made to hold bunches of cut flowers or for growing bulbs.

(left) *Unusual creamware vase, Victorian shape. Printed and hand-painted decoration. Marked: Wedgwood. Height, 13in. [Jo-Anne Blum, Inc]*; (right) *Fairyland vase with waterfall motif as decoration. Height, 8in. [Jo-Anne Blum, Inc]*

It is difficult to find such examples now, and they are so expensive that a collector would hardly dare use them for flowers; but there are many other examples of Wedgwood, Victorian as well as modern, that are available. Nicely designed, simple new Queen's ware shapes, for instance, have been made for holding bouquets of flowers; and many of the old pearlware and Queen's ware serving dishes make particularly good table centrepieces when containing flowers.

Wedgwood experimented with flower holders in order to keep flowers upright in his vases. He designed perforated centre holders which made it easier to place flowers in the containers and yet remained hidden once the flowers were arranged. He gave a great deal of attention to these holders and they were made in as many different clay bodies as was his pottery; later flower holders of basalt, specially those made in the early part of this century, have already become collectable.

94

13
Great Museum Collections

Neither descriptions nor photographs take the place of the real thing. Fortunately for the collector of Wedgwood, there are collections in many of the major art museums of the world. Most of these were originally gathered by private collectors.

One of the outstanding collections is at the British Museum in London, much of which came from two private collections donated to the Museum—The Franks Collection in 1887 and the Falke Collection in 1909. The Museum has, from time to time, bought Wedgwood for display and smaller donations have enabled it to enlarge its collection. It also has a large amount of Wedgwood in storage, which students may see by appointment.

The Victoria and Albert Museum in London also has a great collection of Wedgwood, including some outstanding examples of the work done in the nineteenth century by Emile Lessore. The Museum received a large portion of the collection of Lady Charlotte Schreiber, an extremely determined collector of English pottery and porcelain. Presented to what was then the South Kensington Museum in 1885, the Schreiber Collection contained many examples of early Queen's ware, which Lady Schreiber deeply appreciated.

The largest and most comprehensive collection of Wedgwood in England, however, is at the Wedgwood factory in Barlaston, where the company has set up the Wedgwood Museum, which is open to the public. This museum includes every available example of important ceramics made by the Wedgwood firm since its founding. Josiah Wedgwood's surviving documents, records of production and factory history, and correspondence are all part of this collection, plus drawings and engravings of Wedgwood's early designs.

In many of the smaller museums in England there are collections of British ceramics that include important examples of old Wedgwood. Most of these collections were gathered by devotees who then donated them intact to the museum. Among the most important are the Charles Rogers Collection in the Plymouth City Museum and Art Gallery, the Pocock Collection in the Hove Museum and the Willett Collection in the Brighton Museum. Windsor Castle holds the Royal Collection, a portion of which is on public display in the Wedgwood Room.

America has more enthusiastic collectors of Wedgwood than any other country in the world. Perhaps the finest public collection can be seen at the Art Institute of Chicago. It was the gift of one man, Frank W. Gunsaulus, in 1913, and consists entirely of decorative Wedgwood. The provenance of many pieces in the Art In-

Large creamware centre-piece hand-painted by Emile Lessore. Signed twice by artist on top section. Height, 27in. C1872. [Jo-Anne Blum Inc]

stitute can be traced to many original important collectors of the nineteenth century. The Gunsaulus Collection includes half the collection of Frederick Rathbone, who was a Wedgwood scholar, dealer and writer and whose books are now important collector's items themselves.

The bulk of the collection consists of jasperware of the finest quality with many pieces marked 'Wedgwood and Bentley'. Plaques, portrait medallions, flower pots, bulb pots, vases, urns and the famous Flaxman chess figures are on permanent view in Chicago due to the generosity of Mr Gunsaulus, who was a preacher and lecturer of moderate means and an extremely dedicated collector. He was unusual in that he did not collect for himself but so that the city of Chicago should have an excellent display in its museum.

A small but first-rate collection of eighteenth-century Wedgwood is the Emily Winthrop Miles collection in the Brooklyn Museum in New York. Its quality is exceptionally high, consisting as it does mainly of Wedgwood and Bentley portrait medallions, plus eighteenth-century tablets in basalt and jasperware, early Wedgwood–Whieldon ware and·Queen's ware. The Metropolitan Museum in New York, where the first American exhibition of Queen's ware was held in conjunction with the Ninth Annual Meeting of the Wedgwood International Seminar in 1964, has some fine examples of early creamware and some jasperware.

The largest comprehensive collection of Wedgwood, antique and modern, in the United States can be found in Merion, Pennsylvania, just outside Philadephia. The Buten Museum, founded by the late Harry M. Buten, is the 'Mecca' for the students of Wedgwood and the centre for all Wedgwood Society activities in the United States. Very little of the Wedgwood is behind glass and collectors are able to handle and examine the thousands of items collected by Mr Buten since 1930. If a collector finds a rare piece of Wedgwood, there is usually something similar in the Buten Museum. Other museum collections may stress the early production, but the Buten Museum has examples of all nineteenth- and twentieth-century work as well, besides a library on Wedgwood and related subjects.

The Fogg Museum and the Museum of Fine Arts in Boston are both worthy of note. Shipments of Wedgwood have been unloaded at Boston since the eighteenth century. The Mint Museum in Charlotte, North Carolina, houses the Delhom Collection of ceramics, which includes many important Wedgwood examples.

From time to time there are special exhibitions of Wedgwood gathered from private collections. Many such displays were held to commemorate the bicentenary of the firm in 1959. Numerous owners of important private collections of Wedgwood are willing to risk loaning their favourite items for these exhibitions, though the work of packing and shipping plus the risk of breakage might naturally deter them. Many owners of important works of art, however, feel an obligation to make these available to students and the public so that the work can be seen and appreciated.

Creamware vase. Hand-painted and signed 'E. Lessore'. Marked: Wedgwood. Height, 8½in. C1872. [Spero Collection]

14
How to Display Your Collection

Although Wedgwood falls into two categories, decorative and useful, there is very little old Wedgwood that cannot be used solely for decorative purposes today. For instance, the excellent design and restrained colours and patterns of early creamware, utilitarian when made, now allow it to be used decoratively in eclectic and period settings; and many of the Victorian useful wares may now be used as decorative accessories in less formal settings.

Since there is so much variety in Wedgwood, it is possible to show a number of good pieces without having one's home take on the appearance of a museum or antique shop. It is possible to display a large amount of Wedgwood in one's home and not have two pieces that are similar in shape, design or function. For instance,

Pair of creamware plates with printed decoration in sepia. Marked: Wedgwood C1775 [Jo-Anne Blum, Inc]

(above) *Inkwells and stand in drab colour glaze, hand-decorated in gold. Marked: Wedgwood (impressed). C1850. Length, 10½in. Width, 7in. Height, 2in. [Klamkin]; (right) Coupe shape creamware plate with Sadler & Green transfer print, 'The tea party'. The same transfer appears on Liverpool pitchers. Marked: Wedgwood. C1800. [Schaffer Collection]*

an antique inkwell may be made of Queen's ware, bone china, basalt or any of the other clay bodies made by Wedgwood, and none of these will resemble in any way a pearlware slop jar used as a waste basket near the desk on which the inkwell rests.

When one collects jasperware only, the possibilities for use in room decoration are almost limitless, though one needs to be cautious about colour. For instance, a room where blue is used as an accent colour should have accessories in Wedgwood jasperware of that one colour also. Jasper plaques of the same background colour

Bone-china cup and saucer. Enamelled over the glaze. Marked: Wedgwood (red print). C1815. Diameter of saucer, 5in. Height of cup, 2¾in. [Spero Collection]

take on more importance when they are grouped together. A grouping of plaques, carefully placed, becomes a focal point in a room and gives one's collection more importance than when the tablets are hung at random.

If one has collected old Wedgwood in one colour only, it can be harmonised with the room quite simply by the decorator. Even a comprehensive collection can blend with its background. Basalt items look good in any formal room setting, specially if the background colours are light to set off the shapes and texture of the dark clay.

Often it becomes necessary, however, for the incurable collector to weed out unsuitable items from his collection in order to avoid clutter in his home. The display of a few choice pieces can be more easily appreciated than large numbers of incompatible pieces, no matter how beautiful or important each one is by itself. This is specially true of jasperware.

Many jasperware plaques are bought in period frames. Often the frame is one clue to the age of a plaque, though there are certainly very old tablets that were framed later than the time of their manufacture. Contemporary frames are valuable, and well worth having restored if need be. But pick a knowledgeable restorer. Even Victorian frames will be important some day and should be cared for properly. When having a plaque framed make certain that the frame is properly designed to hold the plaque securely in place; jasperware and basalt are heavy materials and poor framing has harmed many old and valuable plaques and tablets.

Since the nineteenth century was an eclectic period in the decorative arts, it produced pieces of Wedgwood suitable for any sort of home decoration. The neoclassic style of jasperware, made continuously throughout the company's history, goes nicely with the Sheraton, Chippendale and Hepplewhite styles of furnishing and gives more authenticity to the reproductions that are made today. There is much in the Victorian styles, including oriental patterns and elaborate majolica pieces, that are complementary to nineteenth-century antiques or reproductions.

For the decorator, indeed, whether amateur or professional, the choice of decorative items from Wedgwood is unlimited.

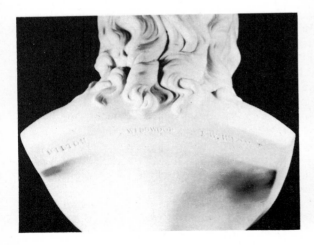

Parian bust of 'The Blind Milton', and marks. This bust was originally designed by Hoskins and Grant in eighteenth century, when it was made by Wedgwood in basalt. The Parian version was modelled by Edward Wyon and was made between 1852 and 1866. Height, 14in. [Klamkin]

Appendix: Wedgwood Marks

The most important fact for the neophyte collector to remember is that **if it is not marked 'Wedgwood', it is not Wedgwood.** Like all rules, there are some exceptions, which will be discussed later, but the 'new' collector should ignore them. Josiah Wedgwood took a great deal of justifiable pride in his product and marked all pottery that left his factory. This practice is taken for granted today and there are laws governing the identification of products made for world trade. However, in the eighteenth century, the choice was left to the manufacturer.

Wedgwood was the first British potter to mark his wares and it is generally felt that he began to do so in 1760, though some scholars believe that the practice did not begin until Wedgwood's partnership with Bentley. In any case, it is possible from the marks used and from other criteria to date certain old Wedgwood ceramics to the eighteenth century or to the early nineteenth. The collector can learn to date Wedgwood by studying the early patterns, border patterns, ceramic shapes, and lists that the factory has of some of its early production. He will also eventually be able to differentiate between the quality of the earlier and later pieces.

The new Wedgwood collector should know the various marks used at different times and on the different types of ware made by Wedgwood; and when he becomes more experienced he should learn the exceptions to the rule that everything was marked.

But in general he cannot be too cautious when it comes to buying anything that does not have a Wedgwood mark on it, There were many potters in Wedgwood's time and since who copied the designs, shapes and clay bodies of Josiah Wedgwood's work and some even copied his mark. While these imitations can sometimes be collector's items in themselves, they are not good investments for the fledgling Wedgwood collector or for the collector with a limited budget. Unmarked Wedgwood may, however, fall into the following categories:

1. Plaques or tablets that were made to be installed in a room as part of the architecture where the back would not have been seen in any case. Examples are chimney pieces and tablets made to be installed in Adam mantels or over-mantels.

2. Intaglios and cameos that were too small or would have been defaced by the impression of the mark. Most of these small items made during the Wedgwood and Bentley partnership are impressed with 'W & B'.

3. A part of a whole, such as the plinth of an urn, the drum of a lamp, or the cover of a teapot, where either the mark would not have been seen or was on another part of the whole.

4. Some pieces of sets of eighteenth-century creamware that simply escaped from the factory without the usual mark. Such unmarked creamware is of value to Wedgwood collectors only when it is identical to marked pieces accompanying it.

Sometimes the impressed mark is obscured because it was not properly impressed in the clay to begin with, but usually the mark or part of it can be found upon careful inspection. Good eyesight or a magnifying glass can be helpful to the Wedgwood collector. Sometimes where the impressed mark is in very small letters it may be hidden by a layer of dirt.

The following is a list of marks used by Josiah Wedgwood & Sons, Ltd, the present name of the business begun by Josiah Wedgwood. The first and oldest marks were impressed, whereas the first printed marks were used on the early bone china in 1812. While impression of the mark in the soft clay has been the standard method of marking Wedgwood until the present day on earthenware, the mark on bone china is printed. Modern earthenware also bears a printed mark quite often along with the impressed mark.

Wedgwood   Lower case mark used between 1759 and 1768.
WEDGWOOD   Used from c1760 to present day.
England   Added to mark from 1891 to present 'Made in England'.
WEDGWOOD & BENTLEY   Impressed mark in various sizes used.
WEDGWOOD & BENTLEY ETRURIA   between 1769 and 1780 during Wedgwood
    and Bentley partnership. Only found on ornamental wares (Upper or lower
    case).
W. & B.   Initial mark used on small items made during Wedgwood and Bentley
    partnership.

Impressed raised lozenges used on ornamental vases, sometimes without the word 'Etruria'

WEDGWOOD   Sans serif capitals used 1928–64.
WEDGWOOD & SONS   Rare mark, used around 1790.
WEDGWOOD   Printed mark on bone china made from 1812 to 1822. Printed in red, blue or gold over-glaze, and sometimes used with impressed mark.
WEDGWOOD'S STONE CHINA   Rare mark found on stone china made between 1827 and 1861.
WEDGWOOD ETRURIA   Impressed mark used between 1840 and 1845.
PEARL   Used from 1840 to 1868 to identify pearlware.
P   Used to identify pearlware after 1868.

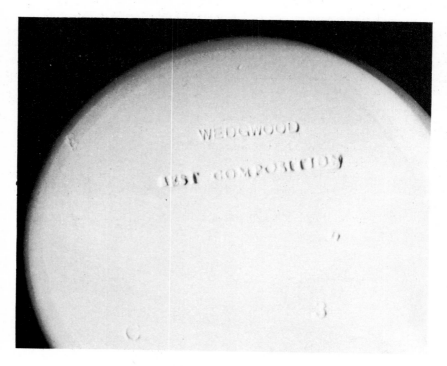

Mark used only on mortars, from 1850

On Wedgwood earthenwares made from 1860 to 1906 will be found a series of three letters in conjunction with the Wedgwood impressed mark. The third letter indicates the year of manufacture.

O—1860	U—1866	Z—1871
P—1861	V—1867	A—1872
Q—1862	W—1868	B—1873
R—1863	X—1869	C—1874
S—1864	Y—1870	D—1875
T—1865		E—1876

F—1877	K—1882	P—1887
G—1878	L—1883	Q—1888
H—1879	M—1884	R—1889
I—1880	N—1885	S—1890
J—1881	O—1886	

From 1891 onward the word ENGLAND should appear with WEDGWOOD (impressed) and the three-letter mark.

T—1891	W—1894	Y—1896
U—1892	X—1895	Z—1897
V—1893		

The following letters are the same as those used between 1872 and 1880, but the word ENGLAND is used on this later chart in conjunction with WEDGWOOD, impressed.

A—1898	D—1901	G—1904
B—1899	E—1902	H—1905
C—1900	F—1903	I—1906

In the above three-letter cycles, the first letter denoted the month in the following fashion.

January—J	July—V
February—F	August—W
March—M	September—S
April—A	October—O
May—Y	November—N
June—T	December—D

From 1907 onwards the three-letter sequence was continued, but the first letter was replaced with a number starting with '3'. From 1924 a '4' replaced the number '3'.

After 1930 a more sensible system was used and is presently being used: in this system a number designating the month starting with '1' for January, a letter indicating the potter (in all cases the middle letter is the potter's identification), and two numbers designating the year. For example: 3 W 42 is March 1942.

Registry marks

Between the years 1842 and 1883 the British Patent Office required a registry mark on British manufactured goods. The Wedgwood firm used this mark to indicate that the design had been registered with the British Patent Office. When this mark appears on Wedgwood items it is in conjunction with the 'Wedgwood' (impressed) mark. If the diamond-shaped lozenge is clear it is possible to identify the exact day, month and year of registration.

In the registry marks from 1842 to 1867, the diamond-shaped lozenge showed the year at the top of the diamond, the month on the left facing you and the day on the right. In December 1860, the letter K was used.

Diamond-shaped registry mark

Month Chart

January—C	May—E	September—D
February—G	June—M	October—B
March—W	July—I	November—K
April—H	August—R	December—A

Index to year in registry mark from 1842 to 1867.

1842—X	1851—P	1860—Z
1843—H	1852—D	1861—R
1844—C	1853—Y	1862—O
1845—A	1854—J	1863—G
1846—I	1855—E	1864—N
1847—F	1856—L	1865—W
1848—U	1857—K	1866—Q
1849—S	1858—B	1867—T
1850—V	1859—M	

In the year 1868 the registry mark changed so that the month appeared on the bottom, the year on the right facing you, and the day on the top of the diamond under the number designating the class.

1868—X	1872—I	1876—V
1869—H	1873—F	1877—P
1870—C	1874—U	1878—D
1871—A	1875—S	1879—Y

1880—J 1882—L 1883—K
1881—E

The month marks used for this second registry cycle are the same as for the first.

The marks for the two periods of bone china manufacture are as follows:

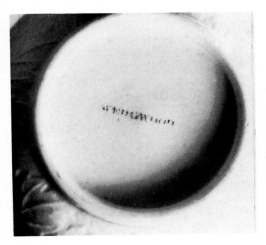

(above left) *Printed mark on bone china, 1812-22 (red over-glaze print)*; (above right) *Printed mark on bone china made after 1878. This mark in gold print is on all fairyland lustre made between 1915 and 1932;* (below left) *'England' added from 1891;* (below right) *MADE IN ENGLAND added after 1898. This mark used on bone china after 1962. Name or number of pattern often added*

Decorators at Wedgwood have always been discouraged from signing their work, but Emile Lessore was an exception. Most of his hand-painted wares were signed, some more than once.

Important tablets and sometimes large tureens are seen impressed twice or more with WEDGWOOD. Norman Wilson's work (from 1927 to 1962) is often signed or initialled. Often the name of the store for which a particular pattern was made in America is printed along with other marks. Plummer's, Marshall Field, and Jones, McDuffee & Stratton are some that are seen often. The latter mark was used between 1879 and 1953.

'Importé d'Angleterre' is a mark that was introduced in 1891

Many potter's marks and initials are found accompanying, of course, the usual Wedgwood marks. Keith Murray designed and signed his wares between 1930 and 1940.

Eliza Meteyard states that the presence in old Wedgwood of 0 and 3 always indicates the best period and the highest quality. Sometimes the two figures are used together and sometimes one or the other is used.

This mark and the one at the top of Page 109 are not *Wedgwood, but are often mistaken for such*

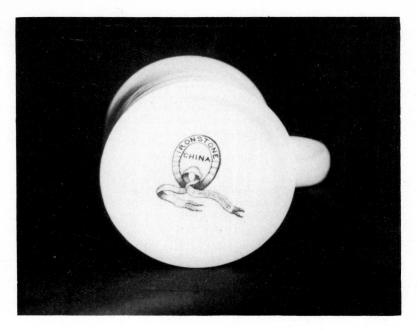

Mark found on reverse of tiles made between 1879 and 1929

Glossary

AGATE WARE—Pottery made to resemble agate stone by wedging tinted clays together so that the colours extend throughout the body.

BAMBOO WARE—Caneware in dark shade shaped to resemble bamboo.

BAS RELIEF—Moulded clay shapes in relief usually applied to a coloured ground.

BASALT—Fine grained, unglazed, black stoneware, made by staining the body with manganese dioxide. Wedgwood refined this clay to give it a richer hue, finer grain and smoother surface.

BODY—Name given to combination of materials from which potter's clay is made. This term is used in reference to earthenware or stoneware.

BONE ASH—Calcined ox bones crushed and ground to a powder. It is the main ingredient in bone china.

CAMEO—Ornaments in relief, usually on ground of contrasting colour.

CANEWARE—Tan-coloured stoneware. Wedgwood refined clays used by previous potters for their buff and brown wares into a lighter body.

CAULIFLOWER WARE—Creamware modelled and coloured in imitation of a cauliflower.

CHINA CLAY OR KAOLIN—Whitest clay known, found in England in Devon or Cornwall, and produced by the decomposition of granite rocks.

CLAY—A stiff viscous earth which forms a paste with water, and is capable of being moulded into any shape.

COLOURED BODIES—Self-coloured body obtained by use of colouring oxides or ochrous earths.

CREAMWARE—Earthenware of ivory or cream colour improved by Josiah Wedgwood.

DRY BODIES—Non-porous stoneware requiring no glaze. Made basically from local clays with additions of colouring oxides or ochrous earths to give the right colour. Wedgwood's dry bodies included basalt, jasper, rosso antico, cane, buff, drab, chocolate and olive.

EARTHENWARE—Opaque ware which is porous after the first firing and requires glazing before it can be used in the manufacture of plates.

ENCAUSTIC DECORATION—Painting by means of a special palette of colours mixed with wax, which is afterwards fused to the ware. It was done mainly in red and white on black basalt by Josiah Wedgwood in imitation of early Etruscan ware.

ENGINE TURNING LATHE—A lathe, equipped with an eccentric motion, built for Josiah Wedgwood by Matthew Boulton about 1763. By means of this lathe geometric, diced and fluted decorations were incised on vases and other shapes.

110

FLINT—Pure silica, the natural stone. It is calcined in kilns and ground to a fine powder. Flint imparts strength and solidity to the body and prevents warping.

GLAZE—Glassy preparation applied to the surface of biscuit ware to render it impervious to liquids.

'Green Glaze'—From 1754 to 1759 Josiah Wedgwood developed the green glaze ware to be fired along with the variegated wares in the common glost oven. This glaze has been made ever since.

'Lead Glaze'—Transparent glaze used on ceramics. At first a powdered lead ore was applied to the surface by dusting and was called galena glaze. Later a fluid glaze consisting of borax, whiting, etc, was developed and is now in common use.

'Majolica Glaze'—Lead glaze stained with colouring oxides to produce a brilliant colour effect. It was introduced by the Wedgwood company in 1860 for dessert services and ornamental ware. The name majolica derived from a type of ware made in Marjorca, Italy, from the fifteenth century.

'Matte Glaze'—Dull glaze without gloss, first introduced by Wedgwood in 1933.

'Salt Glaze'—Semi-glaze or thin deposit on the surface of pottery, produced by smearing the inside of box that holds the clay body with the glazing preparation. This vaporises in the heat of the kiln and settles on the surface of the enclosed ware. 'Smear Glaze' was a development of salt glaze and is often mistaken for it.

INTAGLIO—Sunken or incised design, the opposite of a cameo. Wedgwood made a wide range of intaglios in basalt and jasper for rings and seals during the latter part of the eighteenth century.

JASPER—Dense white vitrified stoneware of nearly the same properties as porcelain. When formed thin it is translucent. It has a fine unglazed surface. The body contains carbonate of baryta. When coloured throughout the body it is called solid jasper, and when the white body is dipped in a solution of coloured jasper it is called jasper dip.

LUSTRE—Iridescent or metallic film on the surface of the ware obtained by the use of metallic oxides, gold, silver, copper, etc. Introduced by Wedgwood company in 1805. The metallic oxides are suspended in an oily medium in which form they are painted on the ware.

'Resist Lustre'—To obtain a more complicated decoration than could be created by simple painting, the resist method of application was introduced. By this method intricate designs are painted or printed on ware with a resist material such as china clay mixed with honey or syrup. The lustre is then applied over the entire piece and fired or fused to the ware. It will not adhere to the portion protected by the resist, which retains the colour of the body. This type of decoration became popular in the early nineteenth century following the discovery of platinum in 1796 and has been used extensively on modern dinner ware, both earthenware and china. Wedgwood's designers, Alfred and Louise Powell, Victor Skellern and Millicent Taplin, combined lustre with colours in free-hand painting. The metallic decoration of the eighteenth century, which has been termed silver and gold lustre, is not a true lustre as known today since the metal was applied with a brush.

'Fairyland Lustre'—Type of decoration used in ornamental china pieces, showing whimsical creatures in fairyland settings designed by Daisy Makeig-Jones in 1920s.
'Moonlight Lustre'—Purple and gold lustre by Wedgwood company as early as 1805.

MAJOLICA—See GLAZE.
MORTAR WARE—Extremely hard vitreous stoneware body introduced by Wedgwood prior to 1789 for the making of mortars, pestles and chemical ware. It resists the strongest acids and corrosives and Wedgwood makes what are still considered to be the best mortars obtainable.
NAUTILUS WARE—Made to imitate the Nautilus shell. The first catalogue of Josiah Wedgwood's shapes compiled in the latter part of the eighteenth century illustrates the nautilus shell dessert service composed of centre bowl, cream bowl and plates. Nautilus has been made in Queen's ware, alpine pink, bone china and moonstone.
ORNAMENTAL WARES—Josiah Wedgwood divided his ware into (1) ornamental and (2) useful.
PARIAN—Hard paste porcelain produced by the casting process. Parian (called 'Carara' by Wedgwood firm) was used extensively by nineteenth-century potters for making statuettes and busts in imitation Parian marble. Wedgwood company first used it in 1849 but never to any great extent.
PEARLWARE—White earthenware body containing a greater percentage of flint and white clay than cream-coloured ware. A small amount of cobalt is added to the glaze for a still further whitening effect.
PIE CRUST—Unglazed caneware made in imitation of pie crust in the early nineteenth century to substitute for pie crust in times of flour shortage.
PORCELAIN—Translucent vitrified ware that has been fired at a high temperature.
POTTERY—Soft, lightly fired, opaque earthenware.

PROCESSES

'Casting'—Process of forming shapes by pouring slip into plaster moulds which immediately absorb moisture from the slip. When a sufficient thickness of clay has adhered to the inside of the mould the remaining slip is poured out and the mould set to dry, after which the form is removed from the mould.
'Dipping'—Process of glazing by submersion in a liquid glaze composition.
'Enamelling'—Segments added over a glaze and given a separate firing in the decorating kiln.
'Engraving'—Cutting of designs on copper plates.
'Firing'—Process of transforming clay into pottery by firing it in a special oven or kiln.
'Glazing'—Application of glaze to the ware, by dipping or spraying.
'Modelling'—Process of making the original pattern or design from which the master mould is to be made. From a drawn design the original clay model is produced with great accuracy and skill.
'Ornamenting'—Process of applying relief decoration to ware while still in the plastic state. Clay is pressed into ornamenting moulds forming different types of relief decorations. The relief is lifted out and applied after moistening the surface

112

with water. The ornamenter fixes the ornament by hand.

'Over-glaze Decoration'—Painting or printing on top of the glazed surface.

'Printing'—Art of transferring engraved patterns to the surface of the ware by means of tissue paper and prepared ink.

'Throwing'—Process of making ware on the potter's wheel. The name comes from the action of throwing a ball of soft clay down upon the revolving wheel. The ball is then centred on the wheel and worked up with the hands. Anyone who collects pottery should try this at least once.

'Turning'—Process of shaping on a horizontal lathe similar to that used in the turning of wood.

'Under-glaze Decoration'—Painting or printing on the fired biscuit before it is glazed.

QUEEN'S WARE—Earthenware of an ivory or cream colour developed by Josiah Wedgwood.

REDWARE—Hard fine stoneware. See ROSSO ANTICO.

ROCKINGHAM GLAZE—Brown and yellow mottled glaze on creamware. It was used to a limited extent by Wedgwood company in the nineteenth century. A shiny brown glaze is also called by this name.

ROSSO ANTICO—Name given by Josiah Wedgwood to his redware.

SLIP—Potter's clay in a liquid state of about the same consistency as cream, used for slip decoration or casting.

SLIP DECORATION—Process of decorating pottery by applying slip over the surface in dots and lines or trailing designs with slip applied through a quill. Similar to ornamenting a cake with icing.

STONEWARE—Opaque vitrified hard body fired at a high temperature, so named because it is excessively hard. It is practically impervious to water without glazing. Stoneware was the principal article of manufacture at the beginning of Josiah Wedgwood's partnership with Whieldon in 1754. Thomas Wedgwood is recorded as making it as early as 1710. It is the connecting link between earthenware and porcelain.

TWO-COLOUR SLIPWARES—Two different-coloured clays used in the same article. The contrasting of different-coloured clays in the same piece is a well known feature of many jasper and Queen's ware patterns. Two-colour slipware is a modern extension of this form of decoration, introduced in 1936.

USEFUL WARES—Josiah Wedgwood divided his wares into useful and ornamental. Useful wares are those to be used primarily in the serving or storage of food.

VARIEGATED WARES—Earthenwares made by the use of different coloured clays extending throughout the body as in Agate Ware or by the mixture of colours in the slip glazes as in mottled, sprinkled, freckled, marbled and tortoiseshell wares.

VITREOUS BODY—A body converted to a glass-like substance by fusion at high temperatures.

Bibliography

BOOKS

Bedford, John. 'Wedgwood Jasper Ware'. Cassell & Company, Limited, London, 1964.
British Museum. 'Guide to the English Pottery and Porcelain in the Department of Ceramics and Ethnography'. British Museum Publication, London, 1923.
Burton, William. 'Josiah Wedgwood and His Pottery'. Funk and Wagnalls, New York, 1923.
Buten, Harry M. 'Wedgwood ABC—But Not Middle E'. Buten Museum of Wedgwood, Merion, Pa, 1964.
—'Wedgwood and Artists'. Buten Museum of Wedgwood, Merion, Pa, 1960.
—'Wedgwood Counterpoint'. Buten Museum of Wedgwood, Merion, Pa, 1962.
Church, Sir Arthur Herbert. 'Josiah Wedgwood, Master Potter'. Seely & Co, London, 1908.
Cox, Warren E. 'The Book of Pottery and Porcelain' (2 vols). Crown Publishers, New York, 1944.
Earle, Alice Morse. 'China Collecting in America'. Charles Scribner's Sons, New York, 1892.
Eastlake, C. L. 'Hints on Household Taste'. Houghton Mifflin & Company, Boston, 1881.
Eberlin, H. D. and Ramsdell, R. W. 'The Practical Book of Chinaware'. Lippincott Company, New York, 1925.
Flaxman, John. 'Lectures on Sculpture'. Bell and Daldy, London, 1865.
Graham, John Meredith, II, and Wedgwood, Hensleigh Cecil. 'Wedgwood'. The Brooklyn Museum, Brooklyn Institute of Arts and Sciences, New York, 1948.
Godden, Geoffrey A. 'An Illustrated Encyclopedia of British Pottery and Porcelain'. Crown Publishers, New York, 1966.
—'Encyclopedia of British Pottery and Porcelain Marks'. Crown Publishers, New York, 1964.
—'British Pottery and Porcelain, 1780–1850'. A. S. Barnes & Company, Inc, Cranbury, NJ, 1963.
Gorely, Jean. 'Wedgwood'. M. Barrows, New York, 1950.
Gorely, Jean, and Schwartz, Marvin D. 'The Emily Winthrop Miles Collection: The Work of Wedgwood and Tassie'. Brooklyn Museum, Brooklyn Institute of Arts and Sciences, New York, 1965.
Heilpern, Gisela, 'Josiah Wedgwood': Eighteenth Century English Potter, A Bibliography'. Library of Southern Illinois University Publication, Carbondale, Illinois, 1967.

114

Honey, William Bowyer. 'Wedgwood Ware'. Faber and Faber, London, 1956.
Kelly, Alison. 'Decorative Wedgwood in Architecture and Furniture'. 'Country Life' London, 1965.
—'The Story of Wedgwood'. Faber and Faber, London, 1962.
Lavine, Sigmund A. 'Handmade in England: The Tradition of British Craftsmen'. Dodd, Mead & Company, New York, 1969.
Macht, Carol. 'Classical Wedgwood Designs: The Sources and Their Use and the Relationship of Wedgwood Jasper Ware to the Classic Revival of the Eighteenth Century'. M. Barrows, New York, 1957.
Mankowitz, Wolf. 'The Portland Vase and the Wedgwood Copies'. Andre Deutsch, Ltd, London, 1952.
—'Wedgwood'. Spring Books, London, 1966.
Meteyard, Eliza. 'The Life of Josiah Wedgwood' (2 vols). Hurst and Blackett, London. 1865–6.
—'The Wedgwood Handbook: A Manual For Collectors, Treating of the Marks, Monograms, and Other Tests of the old Period of Manufacture'. Reprinted by Timothy Trace, Peckshill, NY, 1963.
—'Wedgwood Trio' (including 'Wedgewood and his Works', 'Memorials of Wedgwood', and 'Choice Examples of Wedgwood Art'). Reprinted by the Buten Museum of Wedgwood, Merion, Pa, 1967.
Rathbone, Frederick, 'Old Wedgwood: the decorative or artistic ceramic work in colour and relief, invented and produced by Josiah Wedgwood, etc'. B. Quaritch, London, 1898.
Sempill, Cecilia. 'English Pottery and Porcelain'. Collins, London, 1947.
Taylor, Mrs Robert Coleman. 'Liberty China and Queen's Ware'. Doubleday (private printing), New York, 1924.
Toller, Jane. 'Papier-Maché in Great Britain and America'. Charles T. Branford Company, Newton, Mass, 1962.

PERIODICALS

Buskey, Leo Albert. 'Josiah Wedgwood, Master Potter'. The Antiques Journal, August 1952.
Buten, Harry M. 'Wedgwood Oddities'. The Antiques Journal, Dec 1967.
Chellis, Elizabeth. 'Wedgwood Cameos and Buttons'. The Antiques Journal, 1951–2.
Gregg, Richard N. 'Beeson Collection, Birmingham, Alabama: Eighteenth Century Wedgwood', Canadian Antiques Collector, March 1968.
MacSwiggan, Amelia. 'England's Master Potter—Thomas Whieldon', The Antiques Journal, Sept 1968
Norman-Wilcox, Gregor. 'Mr Wedgwood's Majolica', The Antiques Journal, Feb 1952.
Schwartz, Marvin D. 'Portraits by Wedgwood', Antiques, Feb 1968.
Slavid, Leslie F. 'Black Basalt', The Antiques Journal, June 1953.
Van Tassel, Valentine. 'Majolica of the 1890s', The Antiques Journal, October 1952.
Wedgwood, Hensleigh C. 'Wedgwood on View in London', Antiques, May 1951.
Warren, Phyllis Haynes. 'Lives of the Potters: John Sadler of Liverpool', The Antiques Journal, Sept 1952.

MUSEUM PUBLICATIONS

Buten Museum. 'Exhibition of Replicas of 18th Century Sculptured Miniatures—Wedgwood's Portrait Medallions of "Illustrious Moderns"', 1967.
—'Questions and Answers.'
The Metropolitan Museum of Art Bulletin. Born, Byron. 'Josiah Wedgwood's Queensware', May 1964.
The Mint Museum of Art. 'Catalogue: Delhom Gallery and Institute Exhibition: April 24, 1968'.
Paine Art Center. '18th Century Wedgwood at the Paine Art Center', Kalamazoo, 1965.
Wedgwood Museum, Etruria. Rathbone, Frederick. 'A catalogue of the Wedgwood Museum, Etruria', Stoke-on-Trent, 1909.
Victoria and Albert Museum. 'Cream Coloured Earthenware', Small Picture Book, London 1960.
—'Wedgwood', Small Picture Book, London 1958.
—'Wedgwood Bicentenary Exhibition, 1759–1959', London 1959.
'Wedgwood. Exhibition at Iveagh Bequest Kenwood', London County Council, 1954.

PUBLICATIONS OF WEDGWOOD INTERNATIONAL SEMINAR AND WEDGWOOD SOCIETY

'Minutes of the First Wedgwood International Seminar'. 13–14 April 1956, Philadelphia.
'Minutes of the Wedgwood International Seminar—No 2', New York.
'The American Wedgwoodian'. Published by the Wedgwood International Seminar, Vol III, No 2, Feb 1969.
'Proceedings of the Wedgwood Society', Nos 1, 2, 3, Edited by Geoffrey Wills, London.

OTHER PAMPHLETS

Macht, Carol. 'The Creighton Collection of Wedgwood', Jacksonville, Florida.
McKenrick, Neil. 'Josiah Wedgwood and Factory Discipline', Cambridge, 1961.
Sotheby & Co. 'Catalogue of English Pottery and Porcelain', 24 April 1968, London.

FACTORY PUBLICATIONS

'Talking About Wedgwood: China and Earthenware'.
'Talking About Wedgwood: Decorating Techniques'.
'Talking About Wedgwood: Design'.
'Talking About Wedgwood: Durability and Detergents'.
'Talking About Wedgwood: Jasper and Black Basalt'.
'Talking About Wedgwood: The Portland Vase'.

'Talking About Wedgwood: The Wedgwood Story'.

'Lectures on Wedgwood: Given at the Wedgwood Memorial College, 1968'.

'The Making of Wedgwood', Josiah Wedgwood & Sons, Ltd, Barlaston.

'The Wedgwood Museum at Barlaston', reprinted from the 'Pottery Gazette and Glass Trade Review'.

'Wedgwood Basreliefs, Cameos, Plaques, Portraits and Medallions'. Josiah Wedgwood & Sons, Ltd, Barlaston.

'Early Wedgwood Pottery, Exhibited at 34 Wigmore St, London W1, 1951', issued by Josiah Wedgwood & Sons, Ltd.

'Commemorative Plates'. Jones, McDuffee & Stratton collaborating with Josiah Wedgwood & Sons, Boston, Etruria.

Index

118